To speak for the world

TO
SPEAK
FOR THE
WORLD

Speeches and statements
by DAG HAMMARSKJÖLD
Secretary-General of the
United Nations 1953–1961

Selected, edited and
introduced by Kai Falkman

ATLANTIS

Published with support from
Stiftelsen Riksbankens Jubileumsfond

Atlantis, Stockholm
© *The rightowners of Dag Hammarskjöld* 2005
© *Bokförlaget Atlantis* AB 2005
Pages 235–244, published with permission from
the National Geographic magazine.
Pages 249–255, extracts from *Public Papers of the
United Nations, Volume 2*, edited by Andrew Cordier &
Wilder Foote. Copyright © 2005 Columbia University Press.
Reprinted with permission of the publisher.
Cover: Petter Antonisen
*The picture on the cover is from the United Nation's
archive of pictures.*
Translation assistance: Kim Loughran
Graphic design: Christer Jonson
Print: Nørhaven Paperback A/s, *Danmark* 2005
ISBN 91-7353-063-8
www.atlantisbok.se

Foreword

WITH THE approach of the 2005 centenary of
the birth of Dag Hammarskjöld, the idea
was born of publishing a new collection of
Hammarskjöld's speeches and statements as Secretary-
General of the United Nations between 1953 and 1961.
By replacing the chronological sequence of the 1962
collection, edited by the contemporary UN head of
information Wilder Foote, with short chapters under
subject headings, overview has been facilitated and
repetitions avoided. The choice of subjects was guided
by the importance Hammarskjöld gave to their content
and by relevance to our own time.

In the course of my work I discovered again that
Hammarskjöld did not confine himself to obvious subjects such as the mission of the United Nations, the role
of the Secretary-General, the Security Council's competence and other institutional questions but also devoted
great interest to issues relating to ethics, integrity, duty,
loyalty, neutrality and belief as fundamental values for
international service. Similar issues were thematic in
all his speeches and have a self-evident place in this
collection, not least since they appear to be timeless
and highly relevant through the growing interest for
ethical issues on a global perspective. Young people
seeking meaningful goals for their involvement in the
world around them can find guidance and inspiration
in Hammarskjöld's ideas and ideals.

The texts have been taken partly from Wilder Foote's collection, »Servant of Peace«, and partly from »Public Papers of the Secretaries-General of the United Nations«, four volumes for the period 1953–1961 with commentary by Wilder Foote and Andrew Cordier, close colleagues of Hammarskjöld's.

The texts are largely self-explanatory. In some cases, comments have been inserted to illuminate the context and to provide continuity. In lengthy passages, sub-headings have been included to counteract density and emphasize key themes in the following text.

Dag Hammarskjöld's speeches, statements and writings during his period as Secretary-General contain a rich and varied bounty of subjects, often with memorable turns of phrase, that deserve inclusion in this collection but to avoid bulkiness I have been forced to limit the choice to this, of necessity summary overview of the statesman and private citizen.

KAI FALKMAN

Prologue

DAG HAMMARSKJÖLD was born in Jönköping on 29 July 1905. His father was Hjalmar Hammarskjöld, regional governor for Uppsala province in 1907, prime minister 1914–1917 and subsequently regional governor for Uppsala again until 1930. Dag Hammarskjöld's mother was Agnes, née Almquist.

From several generations of soldiers and government officials on his father's side, Dag Hammarskjöld inherited »the belief that no existence is more satisfying than the unselfish service of one's country – or of humanity.« From scientists and clergymen on his mother's side, he inherited »the belief that in the true, radical meaning of the gospels, all people are equally God's children, to be met and treated by us as our masters in God.«

Dag Hammarskjöld grew up in Uppsala, attaining his Bachelor of Laws degree in 1930. Three years later, he obtained his doctorate in economy at Stockholm University. He entered public service and became at the age of 31 undersecretary of state at the Ministry of Finance (1936–1945).

At the end of 1945 he was appointed economy advisor at the Ministry for Foreign Affairs with responsibility for economic issues. His assignments were increasingly international, including that of Swedish delegate to the Organization for European Economic Cooperation (OEEC) between 1948 and 1953. In 1949, he became State Secretary at the Ministry for Foreign

Affairs and joined the government in 1951 as minister without portfolio. To clarify his non-political appointment in a Social Democratic government, he wrote an article in *Tiden* magazine on »The Public Servant and Society«, spelling out his standpoint:

The basic and self-evident message in the public servant's political ethic is for him to serve society and not a specific group, party or special interest /.../ This fundamental view is deeply rooted in European cultural tradition and has as its most prominent modern representative Albert Schweitzer, who sums up his ethical outlook in the words 'respect for life' /.../

A primary consequence of the view in question is a respect for history's legacy in the result of the aspirations of preceding generations and their attempts at problem solving. This confronts a markedly conservative instinct.

A second consequence is that the political outcome will be guided by respect for the individual, from which derives on the one hand the greatest possible liberty for individuals to shape their lives according to their own thoughts, on the other hand a demand for social validation in the form of equal justice and opportunity for all. This latter point blends liberal and socially radical factors.

Finally, the ethic that Schweitzer embodies leads to an obvious subjugation of private interests to a whole, with a morally based loyalty principally to society but secondly to the greater perspective of society represented by internationalism.

This fundamental viewpoint reflects Dag Hammarskjöld's parental legacy and made him unusually well suited – morally, intellectually and spiritually – for the mission that awaited him.

A neutral civil servant in a neutral nation combined the best imaginable prerequisites for the choice by the United Nations of Dag Hammarskjöld as new Secretary-General in 1953. The French and United Kingdom ambassadors who had first advanced his name to the UN had observed Hammarskjöld's intelligence and diplomatic skill in OEEC negotiations in Paris. Additionally, he satisfied a desire by the French for a candidate who spoke French, traditionally the language of diplomacy.

»From his first days as Secretary-General, Hammarskjöld presented a refreshing picture of principle and intelligence in action,« wrote his close collaborator at the UN Brian Urquhart in his weighty biography of *Hammarskjöld* from 1972. »His confidence, sureness of touch, and strength communicated to others the comforting feeling that in any situation he knew what to do and how to do it, where he wanted to go and how to get there. He was a leader by nature although he lacked most superficial attributes of leadership. His alacrity in thought and action largely obscured the intellectual groundwork that allowed complete command of the most difficult subjects ostensibly without effort.«

Hammarskjöld's public breakthrough as Secretary-General came with his trip to Peking in January 1955 in an attempt to free eleven American pilots and crew from a B29 aircraft shot down during the Korean War. The eleven had been interned in China and in November 1954 were condemned to lengthy prison sentences for spying, which provoked a sharp reaction in the United States. According to President Eisenhower, the flyers' fate was in the hands of the United Nations since they had been under UN command in Korea. On 10 December, the General Assembly gave the Secretary-General the job of attempting to win freedom for the prisoners »through means most suitable in his judgement«.

Hammarskjöld acted swiftly. One hour after the vote, he sent off a telegram to the Chinese prime minister, also foreign minister, Chou En-Lai requesting a personal meeting in Peking. This was a daring move considering that the People's Republic of China was not a member of the UN. Chou En-Lai's answer was positive and he said he was ready »to receive you in our capital of Peking, in the interests of international détente, to discuss relevant issues.«

The talks went well but did not produce a direct result freeing the airmen. On his return to New York, Hammarskjöld explained that the talks had provided an opening for a future solution. Six months later, the prisoners were freed and were able to return to the US.

This was a success for the 'quiet diplomacy' that Hammarskjöld was increasingly to use in a chain of difficult issues to stop public debate and 'grandstanding' locking the positions of the relevant parties and obstructing compromise.

The Suez Crisis of 1956, when France and the UK, together with Israel, without warning occupied the Suez Canal, recently nationalised by Egypt, provided another opportunity for Hammarskjöld. The General Assembly directed the Secretary-General to organise an emergency force (UNEF) under the United Nations to replace the British and French forces at the canal. Hammarskjöld organised the peacekeeping force, to become a new feature of UN activity. The first UN troops were on the ground only two weeks after the Israeli attack and would remain for eleven years.

Simultaneously, a crisis in Hungary erupted when Soviet forces entered the country to quell a revolt against the communist regime. The Soviet Union asserted that the incidents were an internal issue and the UN was powerless against a Soviet veto in the Security Council quashing an American-sponsored resolution calling for the withdrawal of the troops.

In September 1957, Hammarskjöld was unanimously re-elected for a second five-year period. He was able to successfully intervene in crises in Lebanon in 1958 and Laos in 1959, where the interests of the great powers were less articulated. The unexpected attack by France and Great Britain on Egypt at Suez, at a time when they were involved in negotiations led by Hammarskjöld in New York was something of a watershed shock for Hammarskjöld; he had been brought up admiring Britain and France as the bearers of Western civilisation.

Another contretemps with France occurred in the summer of 1960 when French troops surrounded the Tunisian port of Bizerte after President Bourguiba had besieged the French naval base there to force the French to leave. To halt the fighting, which had accounted for the loss of about a thousand lives over three days, Hammarskjöld summoned the Security Council, managing to produce a ceasefire and troop fallbacks. France abstained from voting. Within 48 hours, Hammarskjöld had arrived in Tunis where he could see that France had done nothing to implement the demands of the Security Council resolution. »Bizerte is as important as in Suez,« explained Hammarskjöld in a letter to French diplomat Saint-John Perse, a Nobel Prize winner for literature, »where France failed to uphold the moral principles the West claims to defend.«

Discord with the great powers was further accentuated with the dramatic crisis in the Congo [now Democratic Republic of the Congo, formerly Belgian Congo] following that country's independence. The Belgian colonialists had not prepared the Congolese for the takeover, and continued to administer the country even after formal separation. Belgian officers commanded the Congolese army and the Belgian mining company, Union Minière, continued to exploit mineral deposits in the province of Katanga.

When Congolese soldiers refused to obey their Belgian officers and unrest broke out in several parts of the country, Belgian troops intervened to protect the white population, without the consent of the central government. The situation was exacerbated when the leader of Katanga province, Moise Tshombe, declared Katanga's independence and called on Belgian troops to guarantee law and order in the new republic. The president of the central government, Kasavubu, and the prime minister, Lumumba, turned to the UN for help.

The Security Council was summoned and on 14 July 1960 adopted a resolution calling on Belgium to withdraw its troops from Congolese territory and empowering the Secretary-General to provide military aid to the Congolese government until it deemed national forces capable of fulfilling their duties. The Katangese secession was not mentioned since Hammarskjöld maintained that the UN mandate did not permit involvement in the Congo's internal conflicts. UN troops could act only in self-defence and could not participate in the central government's efforts to re-incorporate Katanga.

Only a day later, Tunisian troops landed in Leopoldville (now Kinshasa) as the first contingent in the large UN operation called Opération des Nations Unies au Congo (ONUC) rapidly organised by Hammarskjöld. The troops used were mainly from African and Asian nations but there were also Swedish and Irish soldiers. Hammarskjöld had wanted to quickly establish a UN presence in the Congo to head off involvement by the Cold War players.

To supervise the withdrawal of Belgian troops from Katanga, Hammarskjöld himself led a convoy of four aircraft carrying UN soldiers. Landing in Elisabethville (now Lumumbashi), Hammarskjöld was received by Tshombe at a well-prepared airport ceremony extensively covered in the international media. This led Lumumba to accuse the UN of sanctioning the secession of Katanga by a »state visit«. The Soviet Union criticised Hammarskjöld for negotiating with »the traitor« Tshombe, and established links to Lumumba.

Political unrest in provincial Congo produced a crisis in government leading to the overthrow by Lumumba of the US-supported President Kasavubu – and the counter-dismissal of Soviet-supported Prime Minister Lumumba by the president. In a country with two governments, each broadcasting inflammatory speeches over the radio, the UN took action, shutting down the Leopoldville radio transmitter and closing the airports. Hammarskjöld had not been consulted but was obliged to approve the measures. To thwart continued Belgian military support for Katanga and Soviet military support for Lumumba, Hammarskjöld requested that all such initiatives be channelled through the UN.

The Soviet Union accused the UN of »shocking colonialist behaviour« and the Secretary-General of being »a conscious tool of imperialist planning and consciously serving the interests of the colonialists«. Soviet opposition to Hammarskjöld's policies resonated in President de Gaulle's statement that the Western powers should have guaranteed cohesion in the Congo rather than »playing second fiddle to the so-called 'United' Nations.«

Hammarskjöld described the Congo situation as a »nightmare«: »a country rushing headlong into dissolution and chaos.« The situation deteriorated on 14 September 1960 when Colonel Mobutu mounted »a peaceful revolution through neutralising Kasavubu and Lumumba«. Subsequently, the Congo was without constitutional government and the Chief of Civilian UN Operations, Swede Sture Linnér, was assigned, with minimal staff and economic resources, to manage and administer the Congo.

Lumumba fled Leopoldville to seek haven in his base at Stanleyville (now Kisangani) but was captured and in

January 1961 sent by Kasavubu to Tshombe in Katanga, upon which he was murdered. The Soviet Union demanded that sanctions be imposed on Belgium, that Mobutu and Tshombe be placed under arrest, that the UN operation be abandoned and that Hammarskjöld be dismissed.

In the Security Council the Secretary-General's only support from among the great powers now came from the US; and in the General Assembly, from the African and Asian countries. The UN's situation was aggravated by the Soviet Union's declaration in March 1961 that it would not share the costs of the Congo operation. Shortly afterwards, France made a similar declaration. This implied that certain states could block majority decisions at the UN by refusing payments – introducing a sort of economic veto.

Sture Linnér took an initiative to improve the political situation in the Congo by persuading the trade union leader Adoula to form a government with himself as prime minister. The UN leadership sought to promote negotiations between Adoula and Tshombe with the aim of restoring national unity. Considering the increasingly reluctant support from the Great Powers, it was of utmost importance for Hammarskjöld to resolve the situation before the General Assembly opening on 19 September.

Hammarskjöld decided to travel to the Congo to meet Tshombe and convince him of the need for reconciliation. Hammarskjöld left New York on 12 September, arriving in Leopoldville the following day. Unfortunately, fighting had simultaneously broken out in Katanga between UN troops and Tshombe's forces, supported by Belgian mercenaries. The meeting became even more vital for Hammarskjöld, the only condition being that Tshombe order a ceasefire. Without waiting for the military conditions to be implemented, Hammarskjöld and several aides and UN soldiers took off in a Swedish-crewed aircraft to fly to Ndola in what was then Northern Rhodesia (now Zambia) where the agreed meeting was to take place.

Hammarskjöld took off from Leopoldville for Ndola in the afternoon of 17 September, planning to be back in New York on the 18th, the day before the General Assembly opening. Coming in to land at Ndola airport at midnight, the aircraft crashed in a forested area 15 kilometres from the airfield. The wreckage was not discovered until 16 hours later. All on board were killed except for a security guard who suffered severe burns and died after three days. The only one not to have suffered burns was Dag Hammarskjöld, who was thrown clear of the plane but died of serious internal injuries.

(An account of the final days in the Congo, the accident and its causes, and Hammarskjöld's documents and notes, is to be found in the Epilogue.)

In Dag Hammarskjöld's last General Assembly meeting in late 1960, the Soviet communist party head, Nikita Khrushchev, condemned UN activities in the Congo and moved that the Secretary-General be replaced by a troika representing the Western powers, the socialist states and the non-aligned bloc. When Hammarskjöld opposed the suggestion, Khrushchev criticised him for not being able to »muster the courage to resign«.

Hammarskjöld's reply, given in the General Assembly on 3 October 1960 became historic: »By resigning, I would therefore, at the present and dangerous juncture, throw the Organization to the winds. I have no right to do so because I have a responsibility to all those Member states for which the Organization is first of decisive importance – a responsibility which overrides all other considerations.«

His words were greeted by strong applause. He continued: »It is not the Soviet Union or indeed any other Big Powers which need the United Nations for their protection. It is all the others. In this sense, the Organization is first of all their Organization and I deeply believe in the wisdom with which they will be able to use it and guide it. I shall remain in my post during the term of office as a servant of the Organization in the interest of all those other nations as long as they wish me to do so.« Here his speech was interrupted for several minutes by a standing ovation.

In that moment, Dag Hammarskjöld was speaking for the world.

Introduction

WHEN DAG Hammarskjöld took office as Secretary-General in 1953, the United Nations was a young and untested organization only eight years old with 60 Member States. At his decease in 1961, the UN had grown to 99 States and today to 191.

Hammarskjöld set to his work as was expected from a neutral civil servant from a neutral nation. Dutiful and modest, he devoted his time to getting to know the Secretariat and its staff, seeking to introduce a regime of truly independent civil service in the spirit of Swedish and British tradition. With firmness of principle he was determined to get rid of all intervention from McCarthy's henchmen who were hunting staff members suspected of un-American activities. He applied his knowledge of international law with negotiating skill and changed the demoralised atmosphere of the Secretariat into a stable working climate.

At the time it was little noticed that he also laid the basis of a definition of the world organization in addresses at American universities and associations. There he formulated the principles that were to be known first after his international breakthrough in 1955 and 1956: First his 'quiet diplomacy' in obtaining the release of the American pilots imprisoned in China ('Peking formula'), then the 'UN presence' of 'peace-keeping forces' in Suez to replace the occupation forces, thereby solving the crisis. Two diplomatic methods, first formulated for students and associations, and – above all – for himself, were now internationally recognized thanks to bold and acclaimed actions.

World organization is a new adventure in human history, Hammarskjöld said in a speech. It needs to be refined in the melting pot of experience. He also described the UN as an experiment in international organization. The UN is something »definite only in the sense that the concepts and ideals it represents will remain an ineluctable element in the world picture.« Thus it was the forms for the high ideals of the UN that Hammarskjöld tried to find through experiments that, if successful, would become enduring elements of international law.

The role of the Secretary-General as an institution of the United Nations was a theme that often recurred in Hammarskjöld's speeches and statements. The chapter on this role is also the longest in the book. Hammarskjöld wanted on one hand to explain the statements and the actions of the Secretary-General to the Member States and to obtain their approval, on the other to lay a basis for the development of his freedom of expression and of action.

As the office of the Secretary-General is the highest authority of the UN, Hammarskjöld said, there is no superior body to refer back to, but »the lack of a such a body does not matter if there is a clear-cut policy line laid down by the main bodies. The lack of means of 'pressure'– if the word is not misunderstood – is in a certain sense a weakness, which, however, is compensated for by the freedom of action, the freedom of expression, which the Secretary-General can grant himself and which, I am happy to note, governments do grant him.«

Hammarskjöld gradually moved forward his position by means of tacit consent. If none of the five permanent Member States of the Security Council intervened to accept or reject a line of action, Hammarskjöld interpreted this as approval and moved on. This often happened with matters outside the direct interests of the Great Powers or matters subject to interests fraught with conflict which they for different reasons wished to avoid igniting.

The Cold War created such vacant spaces, which Hammarskjöld aimed at filling with UN presence in order to prevent other political powers – local, regional or Great Powers – from intervening in the area and drawing it into local fighting or into the Cold War.

CB

When Hammarskjöld formulated the role of the Secretary-General, he first confirmed that the Secretary-General, appointed by the General Assembly upon the recommendation of the Security Council, is above all the representative of the collective of the Member States with a duty to maintain continuous contacts with UN representatives and government representatives of the Member States to form a complete and objective picture of the aims, motives and difficulties of the Member nations. Acting in that knowledge, his duty is to anticipate situations that might lead to new conflicts or points of tension and to make appropriate suggestions to governments before matters reach a stage of public controversy.

The second role of the Secretary-General is to be a public spokesman for the Organization. To explain, interpret and defend the United Nations to the peoples of the world is one of the most important duties of his office, Hammarskjöld said. Surprising is his statement already half a year after his appointment that the most important new factor in diplomacy is mass public opinion as a living force in international affairs. This public opinion has as its background the new mass media of communication, but as a psychological phenomenon and a political factor it is not sufficiently explained by this background. »It is the expression of a democratic mass civilisation that is still in its infancy, giving the man in the street and group reactions new significance in foreign policy.«

Openness to mass opinion implies that the UN »has to operate in a glass house. Multilateral diplomacy is by its very nature such that the old secrecy has lost its place and justification«, says Hammarskjöld. He adds that in the modern world of mass media and publicity, no diplomat trying to respond to the demands of the situations can be only a servant. »He must to some extent and in some respects also be a leader looking beyond the immediate future and going underneath the superficial reactions, be they expressed by ever so powerful new organs catering for what are believed to be the wishes of the broad masses – wishes which may in reality be as loosely attached to the man in the street as the suits which he decides to wear this year.«

Further, Hammarskjöld states that it is part of the diplomat's responsibility not only to lead public opinion towards acceptance of the lasting consequences of the interdependence of our world, but also to »help public opinion become as accustomed to the necessity to give and take and for compromise in international politics as it has long been on questions of state and local concern.«

These are strong words, remarkably far-seeing for fifty years ago. They were addressed to the Foreign Policy Association in New York in October 1953. They imply, of course, also a declaration of intent from Hammarskjöld's side. On the basis of this attitude he accords himself an obvious right – and duty – to address himself to world opinion in order to explain his actions but also to lead this opinion.

In a statement in Washington the same autumn he points out that the Secretary-General »has to try and reach the minds and hearts of people so as to get the United Nations' efforts firmly based in public reaction.«

Here he undoubtedly displays his ambition to assume a leading political role. In a statement before the Security Council in April 1958 on the arms race, he said that »the peoples are eagerly and anxiously expecting leadership to bring them out of the present nightmare.«

The idea of leadership recurs in an address to the University of Lund, Sweden, in May 1959, where Hammarskjöld frankly states that »leadership must be substituted for power – leadership both in giving other peoples their chance and in assisting them, without issuing commands, to find the best way to develop their spiritual and material resources.«

The two rival power blocs cannot exercise universal leadership, only lead an arms race into a global nightmare – this is why the UN as the only universally recog-

nized organization must assume this role. For Hammarskjöld, this represented his duty to preserve a spark of
hope in a very dark world situation.

⚜

Hammarskjöld was a leader of men while lacking most
of the outward signs of a leader, writes Brian Urquhart
in his biography of Hammarskjöld.

As a speaker he generally aroused little enthusiasm as
he read his speeches devoid of dramatic rhetoric, which
he found artificial. When he delivered his historic address in the General Assembly in October 1960 against
the demand of the Soviet Union to resign, he received a
standing ovation, which – according to Urquhart –
embarrassed him.

He soon developed good contact with the press
corps. Unlike his predecessor he did not give individual
interviews, because he did not want to give favours to
anyone. At press conferences with UN correspondents
he generally provided exhaustive answers, often with a
touch of humour, says his personal assistant (1958–
1961) Wilhelm Wachtmeister in his Swedish memoirs
(»Så var det«). He gave the impression of trustful openness without committing an indiscretion or breach of
confidence. Always discreet but willing to present the
background of different political problems, he enjoyed
philosophical digressions. »The journalists were fasci-
nated and imbibed every word,« Wachtmeister writes.

Hammarskjöld was generally clear and pedagogic,
seldom »crystal-clearly incomprehensible«, as was said
about his language of younger years. This phrase origi-
nated from a lack of attention from the listener, explained

Ernst Wigforss, Minister of Finance during Hammarskjöld's period at the ministry. Hammarskjöld had a mathematical precision in his presentations of reports, and if you missed a word the effect was similar to missing a figure in a mathematical equation: the sum made no sense.

Dag Hammarskjöld's language in his speeches and statements have a notable formality compared to the linguistic usage of today. It is a style determined by his position as official spokesman of the world organization but also an expression of the values he represented as a private person. From this perspective the language has an impact relevant also to our times.

His style as a writer of fiction and poetry is very different. It is short and precise, pure and direct, often aphoristic, dramatic in its bold transitions, poetical in its images and compositions of words, rhythmical in its alliterations, assonances and play with spaces.

For Hammarskjöld, »respect for words is the first commandment in the discipline by which a man can be educated to maturity – intellectual, emotional, and moral.« He adds that »respect for words – to employ them with scrupulous care and an incorruptible love of truth – is a condition also for the growth of society and the human race.«

These words are of basic importance to Hammarskjöld and noted in his private diary, »Vägmärken«, translated into English by W. H. Auden as »Markings«. It is to be regretted that foreign readers cannot enjoy the extraordinary beauty and purity of Hammarskjöld's Swedish. I am sorry to say that Auden's translation is often misleading and reveals that he in many basic respects never understood Hammarskjöld. Even the English title is off the mark: »Vägmärken« in English is »Waymarks«, which derives from the Bible, King James version, Jeremiah 31:21: »Set thee up waymarks, make thee high heaps; set thine heart toward the highway, *even* the way *which* thou wendest.« (For further reference see my article on Auden's misinterpretations in The Times Literary Supplement, September 10, 1999.)

ભ

Hammarskjöld based his leadership on the Charter of the United Nations, »the principles of which are, by far, greater than the Organization in which they are embodied, and the aims which they are to safeguard are holier than the policies of any single nation or people.« These forceful words were stated in the General Assembly on 31 October 1956, the same day British and French forces had invaded the Egyptian zone of the Suez Canal.

Taking two of the permanent Members to task placed Hammarskjöld in such a strong state of opposition that he found it necessary to define his relation to the UN organs and their Members:

> The Secretary-General must be a servant of the principles of the Charter, and its aims must ultimately determine what for him is right and wrong. For that he must stand. A Secretary-General cannot serve on any other assumption than that – within the necessary limits of human frailty and honest differences of opinion – all Member nations honour their pledge to observe

all articles of the Charter. He should also be able
to assume that those organs which are charged
with the task of upholding the Charter will be in
a position to fulfil their task.

In plain language this meant that Great Britain and
France had violated the rules of the Charter and thus
prevented the Security Council from acting in a matter
of international peace and security. The Secretary-
General offered his resignation with this final point:
»Were the Members to consider that another view of
the duties of the Secretary-General than the one here
stated would better serve the interests of the Organization, it is their obvious right to act accordingly.«

These words were met by a pregnant silence in the
Security Council. The British ambassador broke the
silence by saying that it was not 'fair play' by the Secretary-General to express himself in this way. Hammarskjöld immediately replied that this was not the right
occasion for the British member of the Council to speak
about fair play. He added that he was fully aware of
what he did.

The situation could be likened to a parliamentary
debate where the prime minister raises a question of
confidence. The Russian and American delegates hur-
ried to declare their confidence in the Secretary-General.
Considering this weight the ambassadors of Great Britain and France also felt it necessary to declare that the
Secretary-General enjoyed their continued confidence.

Hammarskjöld took a considerable risk, emerged victorious and was hailed as a hero in the world press when
he promptly assembled and sent off, with the help of the

General Assembly, the first peacekeeping force of the UN to the crisis area.

The Secretary-General had widened his political powers in a way not foreseen by the authors of the UN Charter. The general appreciation expressed by the majority of the Member States was, however, soon followed by a certain apprehension, as expressed by Krishna Menon of India in a statement at the UN two years after the Suez crisis, where he warned of a situation that would give the Secretary-General a new role independent of the stipulated framework of the Charter.

Hammarskjöld's »steadily increasing activism and initiative set him on a hazardous course between his own sense of responsibility and the interests and sensibilities of the most powerful sovereign states«, Urquhart writes. Hammarskjöld interpreted his responsibilities more and more as a duty to use his position and influence to overcome deadlocks affecting world peace and to keep international problems as far as possible away from Cold War entanglement.

ᏉᎶ

The UN Charter upheld the democracy of states, that is their equality independent of size, political and economic power. This rule was often neglected by the Great Powers. Hammarskjöld went a step further when he placed this democracy on a level with the democracy of human rights – that is, the equal rights of men and women independent of race, sex, language and religion.

Hammarskjöld was painfully conscious of the risk of conflict between these two concepts of democracy. At the same time as he impeded the colonial power ambitions of Great Britain and France in Egypt, he was unable to intervene in the Hungary crisis to assist the Hungarian people in their opposition to Soviet occupation. The veto right of the permanent Member State prevented any 'interference' by the UN.

In spite of this Hammarskjöld considered it unrealistic to abolish the veto right. The United Nations as a whole need not be paralyzed by the veto, he said. »First of all, the application of the veto does not exist in the General Assembly and the other organs. But a more important and basic consideration that should be more widely understood, is that peaceful settlement of the great issues between nations is not prevented by a veto written into the Charter, but by the hard fact that such settlements require agreement and acceptance by the parties to them. This would be true even if there were no provision for a veto in the Security Council. Thus, it is not primarily a question of this or that voting procedure, but of working to create conditions of international life more favourable than those that exist today for the acceptance by the parties concerned of just and wise solutions to these great issues.« In other words, a preventive diplomacy to forestall any conditions that might lead to veto interference.

With regard to the practical possibility of abolishing the veto, Hammarskjöld quotes Krishna Menon: »The day we can get rid of the veto, there would be no reason to get rid of it.« Should the permanent members agree to abolish the veto, there would be such a state of mutual understanding between them that the veto would no longer impede any action by the Security Council.

Almost fifty years later this day has not yet come.

This is evident from the report of the High-level Panel on threats, challenges and change, dated 1 December 2004, which recommends no change in the veto right. It admits that »the whole institution of the veto has an anachronistic character that is unsuitable for the institution in an increasingly democratic age«, but it sees no practical way of changing the existing Members' veto powers. However, new Member States should not be given veto rights.

∞

Even if the Panel does not consider it realistic to implement the democracy of states, it argues that it should be possible and desirable to implement the democracy of human rights. When sovereign governments have proved powerless or unwilling to prevent genocide and other large-scale killing, ethnic cleansing or serious violations of international humanitarian law, there is a collective international responsibility to protect citizens of these states, exercisable by the Security Council authorizing military intervention as a last resort.

Hammarskjöld would have supported this development wholeheartedly. He declared that it was a government's first duty to take measures to safeguard for its citizens the right to security and freedom from fear. But he also recognized it as an »obligation for the world community to assist governments in safeguarding this elementary human right without having to lock themselves in behind the walls of arms.«

Peace and human rights are closely related: »Without recognition of human rights we shall never have peace, and it is only within the framework of peace that human rights can be fully developed.«

Hammarskjöld gave a time-determined definition which is really timeless in the following statement: »The Universal Declaration of Human Rights is an international synthesis of the thinking of our generation.«

»Our generation« has been succeeded by other generations and the continuous development of the thinking about man but with new threats against his rights. After freedom from the anxieties of the Cold War, the right to security and freedom from fear faces a new threat from terrorism, an invisible enemy, present in all civilian populations. »War on terrorism« has, in some respects, corroded the very values that terrorists target: human rights and the rule of law. By focusing on increasing resources for military, police and intelligence measures, the fight against terrorism risks undermining the promotion of human rights. The Panel recommends a series of social and economic measures, with the Secretary-General taking a leading role, to remove some of the causes and facilitators of terrorism.

With terrorism, the spiral of violence grows on all fronts and new fears emerge that weapons of mass destruction will get into the hands of terrorists and criminal groups beyond control, with catastrophic consequences.

ൠ

Hammarskjöld anticipated the widening and deepening of regional organizations. In a speech from 1960, he referred to the recently created European Common Market of six nations and stated that »this system of regional arrangement has been pushed beyond the border of institutional arrangements and has come to include some initial constitutional elements.« He foresaw that the direction of a true constitutional framework for cooperation may, through experimental stages of a confederal nature, finally lead to some kind of federal system or even stronger form of association. He thought, however, that »it is wise to avoid talking of this or that kind of ultimate political target and realize that the development is still in an early stage of institutional evolution, although a few vanguard penetrations into the constitutional area have taken place.«

According to Hammarskjöld it is imperative to push forward institutionally and, eventually, constitutionally all along the line, guided by current needs and experiences, without preconceived ideas of the ultimate form. This is certainly a realistic forward-looking proposition of current interest as the constitution of the European Union is now subject to debate.

As opposed to the European community, the United Nations is a universal community, Hammarskjöld stressed. »In theory it reaches into the constitutional sphere; I have, of course, in mind especially the authority given to the Security Council to act with mandatory power, provided the action is supported unanimously by the permanent members.«

Hammarskjöld welcomed regional arrangements but found it far from realistic to assume that regional arrangements could alone suffice to cope with the urgent problems confronting the community of states. »The UN organization remains the only universal agency in which countries with widely differing political institutions and at different stages of economic development may exchange views, share their problems and experiences, probe each other's reactions to politics of mutual interest, and initiate collective action.«

∞

When it comes to collective security Hammarskjöld preferred to talk about a community of power. As long as collective security was dependent on the Member States of the Security Council, security seemed insecure. Like Woodrow Wilson, the founder of the League of Nations, Hammarskjöld wished to end the old system of the balance of power and substitute it with a community of power.

The game of the balance of power is still inevitable, was Hammarskjöld's pessimistic conclusion in a speech 1956, and he added an interesting remark: »True collective security, in the sense of an international police power engaged to defend the peace of the world, is to be found at the end, not at the beginning, of the effort to create and use world institutions that are effective in the service of the common interest.«

He meant that the spirit and praxis of world community must first gain in strength and custom through organic growth. He encouraged everyone to support these processes by devoting all our ingenuity and effort to realize their success. This shows Hammarskjöld's belief in a creative, peaceful power process instead of a military process of big powers with divided interests.

When Chapter VII of the UN Charter authorizes the Security Council to use military means to maintain or restore international peace and security, this does not mean, according to Hammarskjöld, that it is an organ of collective security of the alliance type, rather that it is aimed at a universal system for the maintenance of peace which may have, as a natural complement, defensive alliances.

When the High-level Panel recommended that in some urgent situations regional organizations may seek authorization from the Security Council for regional peace operations after such operations have commenced, Hammarskjöld might have become wary.

However, the situation in the world is different from 50 years ago, when the antagonism of the balance of powers made such operations risky. On the other hand, nor is the situation today – with one dominating superpower – free of risks, considering that the superpower sees the UN as relevant only when it consents, while the UN security requirements imply neutrality in the sense of freedom from partial interests.

Hammarskjöld generally welcomed regional arrangements provided that they did not undertake tasks that competed with the tasks of the world organization and thus split the world community.

He encouraged Member States to maintain a state of preparedness to be able to meet possible demands for international peacekeeping from the United Nations. On the other hand, the Congo operation strengthened his conviction that the organization of a standing UN force would be an unnecessary and impractical measure, especially in view of the fact that »every new situation and crisis which the Organization will have to face is likely to present new problems as to the best adjustment of the composition of the force, its equipment, its training and its organization.«

For Dag Hammarskjöld it was always important to defend and develop the rule of law against the rule of power. It is, he stated, in the interest of sound development to restrict as much as possible the arena where strength is an argument and to put as much as possible under the rule of law. His daily experience convinced him that »the world of order and justice for which we are striving will never be ours unless we are willing to give it the broadest and firmest possible foundation in law.«

When discussing the development of human society, be it national or international, Hammarskjöld found it useful to employ a sociological perspective borrowed from theories of biological evolution. »It is a perspective which helps us to a more realistic appraisal of what it is we have achieved and are trying to do, as well as of the scope and significance of our failures and successes.«

It was important to get a broader and more organic sense of the role of law, he said, and he used the word in its broadest sense, including not only written law but the whole pattern of established rules of action and behaviour.

Here the resolutions, statements and actions of the United Nations constituted important elements in the construction of an established system of international rule of law. Such a system was, according to Hammarskjöld, above all a guarantee for the security of smaller states, and in extension the security of citizens.

Dag Hammarskjöld's attitude to the primacy of law was a continuation of his father's efforts to create an international order based on law to frame the life of Europe, an international 'Civitas Legum'. Hjalmar Hammarskjöld's work for international principles to govern the states reflected, according to his son, »the conviction of a man who wanted justice – wanted it in realization of how thin the wall is between culture and barbarism, presaging the bitter experience of later decades.«

Hjalmar Hammarskjöld realized that »for a small country, international law, in the final analysis, is the only remaining argument, and that its defence is therefore worth sacrifices even in the egoistical interest of the country itself.«

The defense and development of international law grew with Dag Hammarskjöld into a necessary interest for the world community, worth the sacrifices. A central theme in his private life is the concept of sacrifice, as testified in »Vägmärken«.

⅓

In a speech in New York in 1953, Hammarskjöld referred to an idea from Dostoyevsky's »The Brothers Karamasov«, that the future may be one of a struggle between the State trying to make itself Church and the Church trying to make itself State.

Now, fifty years later, this future seems to be here with states invoking their 'just' belief for propagating gospel and religious organisations invoking their 'just' belief for attaining political power. Our time has seen horrible examples of how both states and religious organizations use violence to promote their ambitions. Big powers neglect the rules of the UN Charter by unilaterally decided preventive war operations against 'evil' states, and terrorists and suicide bombers murder innocent civilians in the name of religion and in the belief that they will receive divine rewards in paradise.

In Hammarskjöld's time ideologies were invoked for the use of violence. The wall between culture and barbarism is thin independent of names of ideologies and religions. Hammarskjöld always said that no nation and no people have a monopoly on truth. Not even the UN has such a monopoly. »The United Nations represents ideals professed by all nations, but it is not a superstate trying to impose on people any 'right' way of life or any way of life different from one freely chosen by the people.« On the contrary, it seeks »as the repository and voice of a common heritage of ideals to penetrate the life of states in their international relations and to influence their conduct toward a wider realization of those ideals.«

ﻌ

During the last years of his life, especially in the shadow of the Congo crisis, Hammarskjöld worried about »subhuman« forces which threaten peace and security on earth. In the midst of all pessimism he still maintained a positive belief in the future as long as there are people of good will who wish to serve mankind. One must not capitulate, he says, because then you betray the future.

»It is my firm conviction«, Hammarskjöld declared in the introduction to the annual report 1959–1960, »that any result bought at the price of a compromise with the principles and ideals of the Organization, 39 either by yielding to force, by disregard of justice, by neglect of common interests or by contempt of human rights, is bought at too high a price. That is so because a compromise with its principles and purposes weakens the Organization in a way representing a definite loss for the future that cannot be balanced by any definite advantage achieved.«

The inner conviction meant for Hammarskjöld a duty to act and to express himself in accordance with this conviction. This was his definition of integrity. It required intellectual and moral courage to maintain this integrity: »courage to admit that you, and those you represent, are wrong, even in the face of a weaker adversary, and courage to defend what is your conviction even when you are facing the threats of powerful opponents.«

Such an attitude exposes us to conflicts, Hammarskjöld admits, but it also rewards us with a source of interior security; for it will give us »self-respect for our shelter«. This position Hammarskjöld defined as maturity of mind, and this is the essence of international service. »It is by striving for such maturity that we may grow into good international servants.«

In 1954, when Dag Hammarskjöld succeeded his father Hjalmar Hammarskjöld in the Swedish Academy, he stated that »a mature man is his own judge. In the end, his only support is being faithful to his own convictions. The advice of others may be welcome and valuable, but it does not free him from responsibility. Therefore, he may become very lonely.«

This was the fate of his father, accused of obdurate
40   self-sufficiency because of his uncompromising policy

of neutrality as non-party prime minister during the difficult war years 1914–1917.

In describing his father, the son often seems to be describing himself, Brian Urquhart notes. Dag Hammarskjöld never belonged to any party or to any self-chosen religious organization – he was an unfettered man, drawing his own borders along the »long way to human maturity«.

The successes of his quiet diplomacy led to criticism of self-sufficiency, even from his closest collaborators, but Hammarskjöld's conviction, based on his experiences, in his ability to overcome antagonisms between parties in conflicts by helping them avoid the often inevitable locked positions of the open debate, made him persist in the method of confidential deliberations.

In personal contacts ideologies could be put aside and positions could be abandoned without loss of face. »You can only hope to find a lasting solution to a conflict if you have learned to see the other objectively, but, at the same time, experience his difficulties subjectively«, he notes in his diary.

The most severe criticism of all tendencies to self-sufficiency came from himself in his unreserved and revealing notes in »Vägmärken«. The price for abstaining from a shared responsibility was the loneliness that dogged him all his life, expressed with despair in recurrent notes.

His work became a flight from loneliness, but after the elevation to Secretary-General, which he interpreted as a calling, his loneliness received a purpose, namely to serve fully and wholly the UN and humanity unreservedly.

The discovery of the ethical philosophy of Albert Schweitzer was of great importance to the young Dag Hammarskjöld. He admired the prominent philosopher and musician for his decision to serve poor Africans as a doctor in the jungle. This decision, and his later exchange of letters with Schweitzer, certainly influenced Hammarskjöld's determination that the UN should be the motor in the development of the new African states into modern societies.

In the winter of 1959–1960 Hammarskjöld made a long journey in Africa which took him to 24 countries, territories and regions during five weeks. On his return to New York he stated that the journey had made him both a little wiser and much humbler. He was acutely aware of the many problems but he was encouraged by his meetings with »the present generation of African leaders of the highest seriousness, devotion and intelligence. I am sure that in their hands those countries will go on to a happy future.« Hammarskjöld envisaged that the UN should play a special role in the future of Africa by providing all the material, social, educational and moral goods that the colonial powers had withheld from them.

Hammarskjöld initially had a romantic view of Africa, says Brian Urquhart. Africa was a newly awakened continent and the UN would proudly take the responsibility of leading the new states to a Western kind of civilisation, which would give them an important position in the world community. But the chaos in the Congo spoiled these dreams.

Hammarskjöld's disciplined habit of scrupulous preparations and rectilinear order made it difficult for him to understand this chaos with leaders who dismissed and murdered each other in a setting of dance, song and great poverty. Worst was that UN troops, sent to the Congo to assist the government in restoring law and order and to effect the withdrawal of Belgian troops from the entire country, were dragged into the conflict as a fighting part. This was totally contrary to Hammarskjöld's stated principles for the operation and must have deeply distressed him. Therefore this desperate and risky journey to the 'heart of darkness', hoping to restore the drama to a human level through reconciliation and peace.

His distress is reflected in this poem: »Do you create? Do you destroy? / These are the questions / for your ordeal-by-fire.« The last word in the Swedish original is »järnbörd«, meaning »iron-ordeal«. It is an old form of divine ordeal. The person accused of a heinous crime had to prove his innocence by, unscathed, carrying red-hot iron in his bare hands or walking with bare feet on red-hot iron. Hammarskjöld died in a sea of fire but he was hurled away from the wreck of the plane and was the only one not burned.

જી

Africa's new awakening and Asia's rebirth were frequent in Hammarskjöld's vocabulary. In his talks with Chou En-Lai in Peking in January 1955 he found an equal in political acumen, diplomatic finesse and cultural knowledge. In a private letter to a friend Hammarskjöld writes that »Chou En-Lai stands out as the most 43 superior brain I have found in the field of foreign policy«. The journey to China was a »fantastic experience« and he writes that in a way he felt more grown up after this.

The change is noticeable also in his speeches. He quoted Chinese philosophers and was amazed by how much more Asians knew about Western culture than Westerners generally knew about Asia. In Southeast Asia he was impressed by the dominating position of religion in everyday life.

During a visit to Nepal in March 1959 he flew in a private plane over the Himalayas in order to take photographs of the largest and highest mountain area in the world. He wrote an essay about his experiences for the National Geographic Magazine, »A New Look at Everest«, which is included unabridged in this book, because it is a very clear and personal description of a unique adventure, showing his versatility as a writer of fiction with swift changes from the concrete to the abstract; his religious thinking with bold associations between Buddhism, Hinduism and Christianity, and his passion for photography with a »hunt fever« in his search for beauty.

In the autumn of 1959 Hammarskjöld wrote 110 haiku poems in the Japanese style, which W. H. Auden describes as one of the greatest surprises in »Vägmärken«. The haiku poems comprise one sixth of the 600 entries in the book, indicating that this poetry was not a passing fancy but a thoroughly tested and expressed form. The poems describe memories from his whole life and constitute a kind of autobiography in miniature. A poem from Nepal may serve as an example: »Sunglittering / the tones of the flute reach the gods / in the cave of birth.« This exquisite mix of light and sound in the cave of birth refers to Buddha's birthplace.

ɔ3

The concept of integrity comprises for Dag Hammarskjöld not only the pure connection between inner conviction and outer action but also the connection of everything in a consistent whole. These two interpretations of integrity are found in Hammarskjöld's exchange of letters with Barbara Hepworth, the sculptor of 'Single Form', placed in front of the UN headquarters in New York as a tribute to Dag Hammarskjöld.

»Your sculpture stands as a sentinel, representing the integrity of both the artist and this operation«, Hammarskjöld wrote to Hepworth after having seen the model. The operation refers to the UN operation in the Congo. The letter is dated 15 October 1960, in the middle of the Congo crisis when the Soviet Union demanded the resignation of the Secretary-General.

The correspondence had started four years earlier, when Hammarskjöld was looking for a sculpture to match the paintings of Picasso and Matisse that he had borrowed from the Museum of Modern Art in New York. He saw Barbara Hepworth's first model of 'Single Form' in wood and found the simplicity and beauty of line and balance quite wonderful. Hepworth replied that she found the same lines in Hammarskjöld's work for peace and order in the world.

They met, and mutual admiration developed in their letters, which more and more took a form that may be described as restrained declarations of love. They were 45 united not only by their similarity of character and ideas of beauty but also by similar generational experiences. They discovered that they shared a most determined aspiration, in different disciplines, to reconstruct a world on ruins devastated materially and morally by two world wars and now threatened by nuclear arms. They belonged to the same generation of fighting optimists with a strong sense of responsibility to create a lasting basis of peace and order for future generations.

They were also alike in shyness and timidity in their meetings. Immediately after a meeting Barbara Hepworth asks Hammarskjöld to forgive her: »I was so deeply touched that I was utterly inarticulate. There was so much I wanted to say – & I said nothing... I cannot thank you enough for those last minutes on Sunday evening – an unexpected moment of 'arrested time' which you invested with a special grace – & which for me has become a charge which I hope to fulfil.«

Hammarskjöld's admiration was expressed in a poem of October 1958 titled 'Single Form', which ends with these words: »The line's light curve / gathers the body's play of strength / in a bold balance. // Shall my mind find / this austere curve / on its way to form?« Their relation had an austerity that demanded absolute fidelity to their inner spirits.

Having visited an exhibition of her works in London in June 1961, Hammarskjöld writes that it was »a sunny moment, full of impressions of perfect beauty, but beauty used as a road to some very fundamental experiences and, if I may say so, expressions of faith.« The letter ends with a promise that »we shall, for our part, continue as well as we can to model in action and words what you are fortunate to express, to perfection, visibly and tangibly.« The »we« is something greater than himself, the United Nations.

Hepworth expressed her gratitude that her work was seen »through the eyes of somebody of immense integrity.«

The last letter that Dag Hammarskjöld wrote to the woman whose beauty of mind and art he so affectionately admired, is dated 11 September 1961, the day before his departure from New York to the Congo. He writes that he has been living with her sculpture in all shades of light, both physically and mentally, and this is his report: »It is a strong and exacting companion, but at the same time one of deep quiet and timeless perspective in inner space. You may react at the word exacting, but a work of great art sets its own standard of integrity and remains a continuous reminder of what should be achieved in everything.« Six days later he was dead.

Extracts from Hammarskjöld's private letters have no place in this book, but the above-mentioned quotations from his exchange of letters with Barbara Hepworth have been included in order to render the deep and wide content of Hammarskjöld's demands on integrity and to show how this person, often described as cool and reserved, was a passionate man when lucky enough to meet another person with the same passion for aesthetic and ethical demands on art and life.

At the unveiling of 'Single Form' in front of the UN building in 1964, Barbara Hepworth said: »Dag Hammarskjöld had a pure and exacting perception of aesthetic principles, as exact as it was over ethical and moral principles. I believe they were, to him, one and the same thing, and he asked of each of us the best we could give.«

Barbara Hepworth broke through Hammarskjöld's emotional isolation. Thereby she integrated him also emotionally with the all-embracing union of the whole that he intellectually and morally had already incorporated into his personality.

ଓଃ

At meetings with the UN Secretariat in New York in December 2004 to discuss the meaning of the so called »Hammarskjöld tradition«, I was surprised to see portraits of Dag Hammarskjöld – a painting, drawing or photograph – on the walls of high officials, next to the picture of the present Secretary-General. The reason, an official told me, is that »Hammarskjöld defined the United Nations and gave it an ethical dimension.«

He told me that, as a young man, he saw Hammarskjöld as a romantic hero who stood up against the big powers, but this image had now been replaced by an image of the international public servant of high moral principles.

Dag Hammarskjöld's idealism serves as a model for young people who now apply for work at the UN, said a woman principal at the department of Humanitarian Affairs: »Hammarskjöld has turned the UN into an organ of citizens instead of an organ of states.« He gave priority to the human rights of individuals above the rights of Member States. »This spirit is still alive in the UN with a lasting impact.«

The Secretary-General who most determinedly has
carried forward the legacy of Hammarskjöld is Kofi

Annan. In his accession speech at the General Assembly in 1997 he declared that »I intend to stress, above all, the moral dimension of our work in this Organization.« On different occasions he has said that Dag Hammarskjöld was the predecessor he most admired for his fortitude and his principled and moral stand.

Like Hammarskjöld the present Secretary-General has been subject to criticism when he has demanded obedience to the principles of the UN Charter, recently from the United States in connection with the invasion of Iraq without the consent of the Security Council. Annan has clearly declared this a violation of international law.

In the spirit of Hammarskjöld he has made clear that »only universal organizations like the UN have the scope and the legitimacy to generate the principles, norms and rules that are essential if globalization is to benefit everyone.«

♋

Was Hammarskjöld a religious man? a high official at the UN asked me. »Have you read 'Markings'?« »Yes,« he answered, and pointed to the bookshelf.

In my briefcase I happened to have a postcard that I had just received showing Dag Hammarskjöld's Library at Mindolo, Zambia, not far from the place of his death. On the back of the postcard was written in block letters a quotation from »Vägmärken«: »I am the vessel. The draught is God's. And God is the thirsty one.« This was written in April 1953 when Hammarskjöld was elected Secretary-General.

In the language of the mystic – we did not talk about 49

this – it means that the I is a vessel which should be emptied from its content of selfishness in order to receive the pure draught of God. And God is thirsty for this drink from man, implying a request to the man who has received God's gift to render it back to God according to his capacity. In Dag Hammarskjöld's words: »The way to holiness in our time goes necessarily through action.«

After half a century it may be appropriate to first introduce Dag Hammarskjöld's thoughts about time.

A confession to a belief in the
continuity of human history

From transcript of extemporaneous remarks at the UN Correspondents Association Luncheon in his honour, 9 April 1958:

> 'The past is always with us and to the coming days we are those who carry the past centuries and also our own few days.'

This poem is written by a close friend of mine who is now dead (Gunnar Mascoll Silfverstolpe, 1863–1942, member of the Swedish Academy, in 'Cantata on the 450th anniversary of Upsala University', 15 september, 1927). I think that is really the way we must look at all our various efforts in the realm of international peace, of the movement towards a world of order and justice.

We have back of us the responsibility created by, in fact, centuries of development. We have in front of us millennia. And in between those centuries and those millennia there are a few years which we might measure in days and weeks and years and five-year terms of office of the Secretary-General, if I look at it from my angle, and those days are really nothing in comparison to what is back of us, and what is in front of us. But they get their sense from what is back of us, and they get their sense in what they mean for the future; that is to say, what we can hand over after our time of work is not just what we have managed to add to the heritage, it is the whole heritage with the little we have managed to add.

It is a confession to a kind of conservatism, a confession to a belief in the continuity of human history, of the history of society, of the history of human endeavour. It is also a belief in the steady growth of human endeavour in a sound direction. I cannot belong to or join those who believe in our movement towards catastrophe. I believe in growth, a growth to which we have a responsibility to add our few fractions of an inch.

A switch has occurred from the mechanical optimism of previous generations to the fighting optimism of this present generation

It is not the facile faith of generations before us, who thought that everything was arranged for the best in the best of worlds or that physical and psychological development necessarily worked out towards something they called progress. It is in a sense a much harder belief – the belief and the faith that the future will be all right because there will always be enough people to fight for a decent future.

I do not think that there is anything automatic in progress. I do not think that there is anything we get for nothing in success. But I do believe firmly that here in this room, around this Organization, in this city, in this

country, in the world, there are enough people who are

solidly engaged in this fight and who are strong enough and dedicated enough to guarantee its success. It is in a sense a switch from the atmosphere of pre-1914 to what I believe is the atmosphere of our generation in this time – a switch from the, so to say, mechanical optimism of previous generations to what I might call the fighting optimism of this present generation. We have learned it the hard way, and we will certainly have to learn it again and again and again...

Conflicts are often never resolved but simply outgrown

From address entitled »The New Santa Maria« at dinner given by the American Association to the United Nations in New York, 14 September 1953:

Time is also a great healer and 'playing for time' is an important element in the tactics we must follow in these days of crisis, anxiety and frustration. We all have a tendency to regard the situation as it exists at any single moment as a lasting one, forgetting that we ourselves and the societies which we form are all subject to the law of change. Those people and nations which are to live together in the future, if we succeed in overcoming the immediate risks of war, will not be of the same generation as those who do not see any possibility of living together as they are now and as conditions are today.

Conflicts, not only in human life, but also in the life of nations, are often never resolved but simply outgrown. Often in history situations have arisen where people were saying, as it is sometimes being said now, that they could neither live together nor fight each other down, 53 and in spite of that, the world has moved on and the situation of despair has become past history.

Failures can in fact be historic steps forward

From address at New York University Hall of Fame, 20 May 1956:

Two of our most common human failings, indeed, seem to be our disrespect for the slow processes of time and our tendency to shift responsibility from ourselves to our institutions. It is too often our habit to see the goal, to declare it and, in declaring it, to assume that we shall automatically achieve it. This leads us to confuse ends with means, to label as failure what is in fact an historic step forward, in general to mistake the lesser for the greater thing.

**Our contribution will lead us to
»the day when joy is great and grief is small«**

From transcript of extemperaneous remarks to the UN staff, 10 April 1958:

Our friends here were singing a Swedish song, the melody of which I think is very beautiful. The words are perhaps a little bit on the sad side. If I may translate the first line of the song, it runs like this: 'Will the flowers of joy ever grow?' Those words, in fact, were taken up later by a Swedish poet, who developed the theme in a way which I would like to mention today as a kind of background for what I would like to say in conclusion. The poem culminates in the words: 'Will the day ever come when joy is great and sorrow is small?' [Gunnar Ekelöf, b. 1907, member of the Swedish Academy, in the poem 'Prästkrage säg.' The song is an old Swedish folk-song and was a favourite of Dag Hammarskjöld's.]

Looking at it in terms of humanity, looking at it in terms of the development of human society, it can be said, of course, that what we are trying to do here is to make our small contribution, during our short time, to a development which will finally lead us to the day 'when joy is great and sorrow is small'.

However, you can also look at those words in a much more personal and intimate sense. I think it is possible to interpret them superficially but it is also possible to interpret them in a sense which goes to the very heart of our way of settling our relation to life. And then I would say that, on the day we feel that we are living with a duty, well fulfilled and worth our while, on that day joy is great and we can look on sorrow as being small…

This poem by Ekelöf was also quoted in Dag Hammarskjöld's »Vägmärken« (Markings) in the spring of 1953 when he was chosen as Secretary-General of the United Nations. After the poem he noted as follows:

It *did* come – the day when the grief became small. For what had befallen me and seemed so hard to bear, became insignificant in the light of the demands which God was now making. But how difficult it is to feel that this was also, and for that very reason, the day when joy became great.

Faith

**The greatest prayer of man
does not ask for victory but for peace**

From statement before the Plenary Session of the General Assembly, 10 April 1953 after his election as Secretary-General:

We are of different creeds and convictions. Events and ideas which to some of us remain the very basis of our faith are elements of the spiritual heritage of man which are foreign to others. But common to us all, and above all other convictions stands the truth, once expressed by a Swedish poet when he said that the greatest prayer of man does not ask for victory but for peace. (Erik Axel Karlfeldt 1864–1931, member of the Swedish Academy, awarded the Nobel Prize in Literature, 1931.)

**The »self-surrender« of medieval mystics has become
the way to self-realization in an unhesitant fulfillment
of duty and in an unreserved acceptance of life**

*Written for Edward R. Murrow's radio programme »This I Believe«
in 1954:*

The world in which I grew up was dominated by principles and ideals of a time far from ours and, as it may seem, far removed from the problems facing a man of the twentieth century. However, my way has not meant a departure from those ideals. On the contary, I have been led to an understanding of their validity also for our world of today. Thus, a never abandoned effort frankly and squarely to build up a personal belief in the light of experience and honest thinking has led me in a circle; I now recognize and endorse, unreservedly, those very beliefs which were once handed down to me.

From generations of soldiers and government officials on my father's side I inherited a belief that no life was more satisfactory than one of selfless service to your country – or humanity. This service required a sacrifice of all personal interests, but likewise the courage to stand up unflinchingly for your convictions.

From scholars and clergymen on my mother's side I inherited a belief that, in the very radical sense of the Gospels, all men were equals as children of God, and should be met and treated by us as our masters in God.

Faith is a state of the mind and the soul. In this sense we can understand the words of the Spanish mystic, St. John of the Cross: »Faith is the union of God with the soul.« The language of religion is a set of formulas which register a basic spiritual experience. It must not be regarded as describing, in terms to be defined by philosophy, the reality which is accessible to our senses and which we can analyse with the tools of logic. I was late in understanding what this meant. When I finally reached that point, the beliefs in which I was once brought up and which, in fact, had given my life direction even while my intellect still challenged their validity, were recognized by me as mine in their own right and by my free choice. I feel that I can endorse those convictions without any compromise with the demands of that intellectual honesty which is the very key to maturity of

mind.

The two ideals which dominated my childhood world I came upon fully harmonized and adjusted to the demands of our world of today in the ethics of Albert Schweitzer, where the ideal of service is supported by and supports the basic attitude to man set forth in the Gospels. In his work I also found a key for modern man to the world of the Gospels.

But the explanation of how man should live a life of active social service in full harmony with himself as a member of the community of the spirit, I found in the writings of those great medieval mystics for whom 'self-surrender' had been the way to self-realization, and who in 'singleness of mind' and 'inwardness' had found strength to say *yes* to every demand which the needs of their neighbours made them face, and to say *yes* also to every fate life had in store for them when they followed the call of duty as they understood it. Love – that much misused and misinterpreted word – for them meant simply an overflowing of the strength with which they felt themselves filled when living in true self-oblivion. And this love found natural expressions in an unhesitant fulfillment of duty and in an unreserved acceptance of life, whatever it brought them personally of toil, suffering – or happiness.

I know that their discoveries about the laws of inner life and action have not lost their significance.

The United Nations stands outside all confessions but is nevertheless an instrument of faith

From address entitled »An Instrument of Faith« given to Assembly of World Council of Churches, 20 August 1954:

The Churches are guardians of and spokespeople for the deepest beliefs and the loftiest dreams of man. The United Nations, on the other hand, is an organization for continuous diplomatic negotiation concerning concrete political issues, providing also for international administrative action in the economic and social fields.

Yet, in spite of all differences in character and responsibility, the Churches and the United Nations have an aim in common and a field of action where they work side by side.

In a televised interview some time ago, a youngster of sixteen asked me with concern why there is no reference to God in the United Nations Charter. In my reply I drew his attention to the Preamble of the Charter where the nations express their 'faith in the dignity and worth of the human person' and pledge themselves 'to practice tolerance and live together in peace with one another as good neighbours'. I felt sure that he saw here an expression of what, in the faith which was his, was recognized as the will of God: that we should love our neighbours as ourselves. He could not expect a document which should serve as a basis for world cooperation to go further in the direction he had in mind. The United Nations must recognize and respect all the different creeds and attitudes represented by its Member nations.

The question and my reply emphasize some basic facts. The United Nations stands outside – necessarily outside – all confessions but it is, nevertheless, an instrument of faith. As such it is inspired by what unites and not by what divides the great religions of the world.

In the same spirit it may be said of the United Nations that what is required from the Organization – and from the governments and peoples therein represented – is a renewed faith, a faith renewed every day, expressed in a never abandoned, every day newly initiated, responsible action for peace.

Thus, in spite of their different roles in the life of the community and the peoples, the Organization and the Churches stand side by side as participants in the efforts of all men of good will, irrespective of their creed or form of worship, to establish peace on earth.

The hope for a world of peace and order has never ceased to agitate the minds of men

From address at Stanford University, 19 June 1955:

Every nation has its heroes, its martyrs and its saints. The world also has its heroes and saints. One who long ago spoke among a small, oppressed people for the brotherhood of all men was sacrificed as a danger to the safety of his own nation. Western civilization has aspired for nearly 2 000 years to follow the life and teachings of this apostle of peace. But all through those 2 000 years nationalism in the narrow and dangerous sense of the word has remained a major force. In the light of history, one might well ascribe to mankind the words of Milton's Lucifer: 'For only in destroying I find ease to my relentless thoughts.'

The cynic may well ask: where in the political and national histories of this period do we see a reflection of the creed professed by sovereigns and peoples alike? The cynic may also say that as the past has been, so will the future be. It is my belief that he is wrong on both scores. Whatever doubts history may cast, I believe that the hope for a world of peace and order, inspired by respect for man, has never ceased to agitate the minds of men. I believe that it accounts for the great and noble human spirit behind the ravaged exterior of a history whose self-inflicted wounds have become more and more atrocious. And I believe that at the point we have now reached in our technical development, our creed may gain new possibilities to shape history. A faith like that which has inspired the spiritual life of the West could seem only a dream to the leader of the people of a powerful nation which can dominate others, or considers itself untouched by their actions. There is a new situation the day you have to recognize that you cannot dictate to other nations and that you are not independent of the actions of other nations. It is more difficult to see your brother in a slave or a master. It is easier to see him in somebody with whom you have to live without giving or taking orders. Looking back into the past we see how peoples have been oppressed – and how peoples have accepted oppression – in the name of God. May we not be approaching a time when in His name they will instead be giving and accepting freedom?

The international public servant

**The international public servant assists those
who take decisions which frame history**

*From statement to the press on arrival at New York International
Airport, 9 April 1953:*

In my new official capacity the private man should dis-
appear and the international public servant take his
place. The public servant is there in order to assist, so to
say from the inside, those who take the decisions which
frame history. He should – as I see it – listen, analyze
and learn to understand fully the forces at work and the
interests at stake, so that he will be able to give the right
advice when the situation calls for it. Don't think that he
– in following this line of personal policy – takes but a
passive part in the development. It is a most active one.
But he is active as an instrument, a catalyst, perhaps an
inspirer – he serves.

**International service requires
the courage to be ourselves**

*From address at Johns Hopkins University in Baltimore, 14 June
1955:*

At this time of great ideological conflicts and violent
clashes of interests, technological and economic developments have, as never before, brought us together as
members of one human family, unified beyond race or 63

creed on a shrinking globe, in the face of dangers of our own making. In such a situation many ethical problems take on a new significance and our need to give sense to our lives exceeds the inherited standards. True, our duties to our families, our neighbours, our countries, our creeds have not changed. But something has been added. This is a duty to what I shall call international service, with a claim on our lives equal to that of the duty to serve within those smaller units whose walls are now breaking down. The international service of which I speak is not the special obligation, nor the privilege, of those working in international economic corporations, in the field of diplomacy, or in international political organizations. It has become today the obligation, as well as the privilege, of all.

International service requires of all of us first and foremost the courage to be ourselves. In other words, it requires that we should be true to none other than our ideals and interests – but these should be such as we can fully endorse after having opened our minds, with great honesty, to the many voices of the world. The greatest contribution to international life that any one can render – be it as a private citizen or as one professionally engaged in international work – is to represent frankly and consistently what survives or emerges as one's own after such a test. Far from demanding that we abandon or desert ideals and interests basic to our personality, international service thus puts us under the obligation to let those ideals and interests reach maturity and fruition in a universal climate.

Maturity of mind is the essence of international service

If this is the essence of international service, such service will expose us to conflicts. It will not permit us to live lazily under the protection of inherited and conventional ideas. Intellectually and morally, international service therefore requires the courage to admit that you, and those you represent, are wrong, when you find them to be wrong, even in the face of a weaker adversary, and courage to defend what is your conviction even when you are facing the threats of powerful opponents. But while such an outlook exposes us to conflicts, it also provides us with a source of inner security; for it will give us 'self-respect for our shelter'. This is, as you may remember, the privileged position which Epictetus grants to the Cynic when he, true to his ideals, sacrifices all outward protection.

In the flourishing literature on the art of life there is much talk about that rare quality: maturity of mind. It is easy to circumscribe such maturity in negative terms. In positive terms it is difficult to define it, although we all recognize it when we have the privilege of seeing its fruits. It is reflected in an absence of fear, in recognition of the fact that fate is what we make it. It finds expression in an absence of attempts to be anything more than we are, or different from what we are, in recognition of the fact that we are on solid ground only when we accept giving to our fellow men neither more nor less than what is really ours. You yourselves can complete the picture. Maturity of mind seems to me to be the very basis for that attitude which I have described here as the essence of international service. It is by striving for such maturity that we may grow into good international servants.

A growing group of men all over the world regard service to fellow members of mankind to be a reward in itself

From statement before the General Assembly, 17 October 1960:

Those many men, from many nations in Africa, Asia, Europe and the transatlantic countries, who are serving the United Nations in the Congo, why are they there? May I pay them a tribute as pioneers for that growing group of men all over the world who regard service to the fellow members of the community of mankind to be a reward in itself, giving sense to their efforts and to their life – guided by faith in a better future and maintaining the strict norms of behavior which the Charter requests of an international civil servant. Blame them for their shortcomings if you will; say that they should do more if you believe that you are entitled to say so; criticize this or that decision they have taken, because in your perspective another decision might have been better, but do not throw doubt on their honesty and seriousness, do not impugn their motives and, especially, do not try to depict them as enemies of the very cause – the well-being of the Congolese people in a life of peace and true independence – for which they are giving so much and, in worldly terms, as individuals, receiving little or nothing.

Extracts from Hammarskjöld's famous lecture entitled »The International Civil Servant in Law and in Fact« at Oxford University, 30 May 1961, are to be found in the chapters on »The role of the Secretary-General« and »Neutral and Neutrality«.

The United Nations

**World organization is a new
adventure in human history**

Extract from address at New York University, 20 May 1956:

When he opened discussion of plans for a League of
Nations at the Paris Peace Conference in January 1919,
Wilson called for the creation of an organization that
should, he stressed, be 'not merely a formal thing, not
an occasional thing, not a thing sometimes called into
life to meet an exigency' but that should have a 'vital
continuity' of function. He summed it up in these ex-
pressive words: 'It should be the eye of the nations to
keep watch upon the common interest, an eye that does
not slumber, an eye that is everywhere watchful and
attentive.' Forty years after Woodrow Wilson first
uttered these words, the idea of world organization is
far more firmly established than it ever was in the years
of the League of Nations. The mere fact that the United
Nations, unlike the League, has never lost a Member
state, and now, with seventy-six Members, seems to be
moving inexorably towards true universality, speaks for
this. But we are still seeking ways to make our international institutions fulfill more effectively the fundamental purpose expressed in Woodrow Wilson's words – 'to
be the eye of the nations to keep watch upon the common interest'.

I have no doubt that forty years from now we shall

also be engaged in the same pursuit. How could we expect otherwise? World organization is still a new adventure in human history. It needs much perfecting in the crucible of experience and there is no substitute for time in that respect.

Embodiment of the groping efforts of mankind towards an organized world community

From address at the American Jewish Committee, New York, 10 April 1957:

The United Nations finds itself in a difficult stage of its development. It is still too weak to provide the security desired by all, while being strong enough and alive enough effectively to point out the direction in which the solution must be sought. In its present phase the Organization may look to many like a preacher who cannot impose the law he states or realize the gospel he interprets.

It is easy to say that it is pointless to state the law if it cannot be enforced. However, to do so is to forget that if the law is the inescapable law of the future, it would be treason to the future not to state the law simply because of the difficulties of the present. Indeed, how could it ever become a living reality if those who are responsible for its development were to succumb to the immediate difficulties arising when it is still a revolutionary element in the life of society?/.../

They apply likewise to the United Nations itself as an experiment in international organization. But is not an experiment something tentative and passing? And should not the United Nations be regarded as something definite and lasting? I think it is important to be clear on this point. Certainly the experiences and achievements of the United Nations as it is today are helping us to build the future. The United Nations is something definite also in the sense that the concepts and ideals it represents, like the needs it tries to meet, will remain an ineluctable element of the world picture. However, that does not mean that the present embodiment of the groping efforts of mankind towards an organized world community represents a definite shape selection, or out of experience. Thus an effort that has not yielded all the results hoped for has not failed if it has provided positive experience on which a new approach can be based. An attempt which has proved the possibility of progress has served the cause of progress even if it has had to be renewed again and again, and in new forms or settings in order to yield full success.

The diplomacy of reconciliation of the United Nations serves better than other instruments available to the Member States

From Introduction to the Annual Report 1956–1957:

We should, rather, recognize the United Nations for what it is – an admittedly imperfect but indispensable instrument of nations in working for a peaceful evolution towards a more just and secure world order. The dynamic forces at work in this stage of human history have made world organization necessary. The balance of these forces has also set the limits within which the power of world organization can develop at each step and beyond which progress, when the balance of forces 69 so permits, will be possible only by processes of organic growth in the system of custom and law prevailing in the society of nations.

These processes of adjustment take time. Systems of alliance, maintained side by side with the United Nations in recognition of the prevailing balance of forces, may serve a useful purpose during the period through which we are passing. However, most of us agree that such systems of alliance, like other traditional means of diplomacy and defense of the national interest, are limited in their value as safeguards of the present and future security and welfare of our countries. Nations and groups of nations will never again be able to live and to arrogate judgment unto themselves in international affairs in ways which once were a matter of course.

The greatest need today is to blunt the edges of conflict among the nations, not to sharpen them. If properly used, the United Nations can serve a diplomacy of reconciliation better than other instruments available to the Member States. All the varied interests and aspirations of the world meet in its precincts upon the common ground of the Charter. Conflicts may persist for long periods without an agreed solution and groups of States may actively defend special and regional interests. Nevertheless, and in spite of temporary developments in the opposite direction under the influence of acute tension, the tendency in the United Nations is to wear away, or break down, differences, thus helping toward solutions which approach the common interest and application of the principles of the Charter.

Any compromise with the principles and purposes of the United Nations results in a weakening of the confidence in the Organization and in a loss for the future

From Introduction to the Annual Report 1959–1960:

Finally, the Organization is also the embodiment of an ideal and the symbol of an approach to international life which recognizes the common interest of all in the rejection of the use of force, in any form, as a means for settling disputes and in adherence to the principles of law, justice, and human rights.

The Organization has often in the past been faced, and is likely in its continued work again and again to be faced, with situations in which a compromise with these last-mentioned principles might seem to facilitate the achievement of results in negotiations or to promise an easier success for the Organization in its executive efforts to resolve a problem. It is for the Members themselves to judge to what extent the Organization, in particular cases, has accepted such compromises and to what extent it has remained faithful to the principles and ideals which it embodies.

It is my firm conviction that any result bought at the price of a compromise with the principles and ideals of the Organization, either by yielding to force, by disregard of justice, by neglect of common interests or by contempt for human rights, is bought at too high a price. That is so because a compromise with its principles and purposes weakens the Organization in a way representing a definite loss for the future that cannot be balanced by any immediate advantage achieved /.../

It is impossible for anyone to say where the international community is heading and how the United Nations will change in the further course of evolution of international politics. But it can safely be said that international cooperation will become increasingly essential for the maintenance of peace, progress and international justice. It can also safely be said that if the United Nations firmly adheres to its principles and purposes, with flexibility and intelligent adjustment to needs as regards procedure, Members engaged in this cooperation will increasingly turn to the Organization for assistance. Therefore, they will find it increasingly necessary to maintain its strength as an instrument for the world community in their efforts to reduce those areas of major conflict where the Organization so far has been powerless, as well as in efforts to resolve problems, arising outside or on the margin of these areas, in a spirit reflecting the overriding common interest.

The role of the Secretary-General

**Consultant to the governments outside publicity
as well as public spokesman for the United Nations**

*From address to American Association for the United Nations,
New York, 14 September 1953:*

I do not conceive the role of the Secretary-General and
the Secretariat as representing what has been called a
'third line' in the international debate. Nor is it for him
to try and initiate 'compromises' that might encroach
upon areas that should be exclusively within the sphere
of responsibility of the respective national governments.

On the other side I see the duty of the Secretariat to
form, in the first instance, a most complete and objective picture of the aims, motives and difficulties of the
Member nations. Acting in that knowledge, it is our
duty to seek to anticipate situations that might lead to
new conflicts or points of tension and to make appropriate suggestions to the governments before matters reach
a stage of public controversy.

Beyond this, the Secretary-General should express
with full frankness to the governments concerned and
their representatives the conclusions at which he arrives
on issues before the Organization. These conclusions
must be completely detached from any national interest
or policy and based solely on the principles and ideals to
which the governments have adhered as Members of the
United Nations. In other words, the relationship of the

Secretary-General to the governments should be one of a trusted consultant on those considerations following from adherence to the Charter and membership in the United Nations that should be taken into account by the governments in coming to their own policy decisions.

Clearly such a relationship of mutual confidence and trust would be impossible in an atmosphere of publicity. This does not mean that the Secretary-General should not also be a public spokesman for the Organization. Indeed, to explain, interpret and defend the United Nations to the peoples of the world is one of the important duties of his office. But he should never do this in such a way as to contravene his obligations as representative of all Member nations and to the principles of the Organization. He should not permit himself to become a cause of conflict unless the obligations of his office under the Charter and as an international civil servant leave him no alternative.

The freedom of action and of expression which the Secretary-General can grant himself

From press conference comments, 4 April 1957:

On the other hand he [the Secretary-General] finds himself in a situation where he lacks not means of pressure, but the kind of weight which every government necessarily has because it is part of the world picture, part of the whole pattern of trade, policy-making and so on and so forth. That is partly compensated for by one fact. Because he has no pressure group behind him, no territory and no parliament in the ordinary sense of the word, he can talk with much greater freedom, much greater frankness and much greater simplicity in approaching governments than any government representative can do. In summing up, I would say that the lack of a superior body to which to refer does not matter if there is a clear-cut policy line laid down by the main bodies here. The lack of means of 'pressure' – if the word is not misunderstood – is in a certain sense a weakness which, however, is compensated for by the freedom of action, the freedom of expression, which the Secretary-General can grant himself and which, I am happy to note, governments do grant him.

The evolution of the office of the Secretary-General reflects a growth of possibilities for the United Nations to operate within a higher degree of independence

From Introduction to the Annual Report 1958–1959:

In considering the evolution of procedures of the principal United Nations organs, attention may also be given to the developing functions of the Secretariat. There have been, in the first place, various decisions taken in recent years by the General Assembly or the Security Council under which the Secretary-General has been entrusted with special diplomatic and operational functions, which he is responsible for carrying out within the wide framework of general terms of reference laid down in the resolutions and, naturally, in the Charter itself. This, also, represents an evolution of the procedures of the United Nations for which no explicit basis is to be found in the Charter – although it may be said to fall within the scope of the intentions reflected in Article 99* – and to which neither the League of Nations, nor the United Nations during its earlier years, presented a significant counterpart. These decisions should not, of course, be considered as setting precedents changing the constitutional balance among the various organs of the United Nations. However, they have pointed to the possibility of developing new methods of approach of great practical significance, which, after the thorough testing needed, may become part of a common law of organized international cooperation.

It should also be noted that in some recent cases of international conflict or other difficulties involving Member States the Secretary-General has dispatched personal representatives with the task of assisting the governments in their efforts. This may be regarded as a further development of actions of a 'good offices' nature, with which the Secretary-General is now frequently charged. The steps to which I refer here have been taken with the consent or at the invitation of governments concerned, but without formal decisions of other organs of the United Nations. Such actions by the Secretary-General fall within the competence of his office and are, in my view, in other respects also in strict accordance with the Charter, when they serve its purpose. As a matter of course, the members of the appropriate organ of the United Nations have been informed about the action planned by the Secretary-General and were given an opportunity to express views on it. These cases also should not be considered as setting precedents, especially as it always remains open to the appropriate organs to request that such an action, before being taken by the Secretary-General, be submitted to them for formal decision. However, in these cases too, what has been tried may provide experiences on which, later, stable and agreed practices may usefully be developed.

The main significance of the evolution of the office of

the Secretary-General in the manner referred to above lies in the fact that it has provided means for smooth and fast action, which might otherwise not have been open to the Organization. This is of special value in situations in which prior public debate on a proposed course of action might increase the difficulties that such an action would encounter, or in which a vacuum might be feared because Members may prove hesitant, without fuller knowledge of the facts or for other reasons, to give explicit prior support in detail to an action which, however, they approve in general terms or are willing should be tried without formal commitment.

It goes without saying that none of the developments to which I have referred has changed the basic character of the office of the Secretary-General, or its place in the Organization in relation to the General Assembly, the Security Council or other main organs. They represent, from a constitutional viewpoint, an intensification and a broadening of the interplay between these main organs and the Secretariat for purposes for which these organs maintain their primary responsibility. Thus, the wider functions which in specific cases have been exercised by the Secretary-General, fully maintain the character of the United Nations as an organization whose activities are wholly dependent on decisions of the governments. On the other hand, the development reflects an incipient growth of possibilities for the Organization to operate in specific cases within a latitude of independence in practice given to it by its Member governments for such cases.

*Under Article 99 »The Secretary-General may bring to the attention of the Security Council any matter which in his opinion may threaten the maintenance of international peace and security«. In his statements at the time of the 1956 Suez and Hungarian crises Dag Hammarskjöld informed the Security Council that he would have invoked Article 99 if the United States had not acted first to bring the issues before the Council. Article 99 was first formally invoked in the Congo crisis in 1960.

Working at the edge of the development of human society is to work on the brink of the unknown

From address at University of Chicago, 1 May 1960:

The Secretary-General of the United Nations is the Chief Administrative Officer of the Organization and, as such, the only elected member of the Secretariat. The founders of the United Nations may in this context have looked to the American Constitution. The chief of any government, or the Chief Executive in the United States, has the assistance of a group of close collaborators who represent the same basic approach, and to whom he therefore can delegate a considerable part of his responsibilities. On the basis of universality, especially in a divided world but generally speaking as long as nations have opposing interests, no similar arrangement is possible within the United Nations. This may have been understood in San Francisco, but I guess that it was felt that it did not matter too much as the Secretary-General had mainly administrative responsibilities. However, the position of the Office of the Secretary-General within the United Nations, explained in part by the fact that he is the only elected officer in principle representing all members, has led to increasingly widespread diplomatic and political activities. This is in response to developing needs. If negotiations are necessary, or if arrangements with a certain intended political impact are to be made, but Member nations are not in a position to lay down exact terms of reference, a natural response of the Organization is to use the services of the Secretary-General for what they may be worth.

The tasks thus entrusted to the Secretary-General are mostly of such a character that, with the composition of an international Secretariat and of the group of his closest collaborators, with its naturally wide geographical distribution, he must carry out the work on a fairly personal basis. Obviously, there is no parallel to this in the field of national politics or diplomacy, and the case I have described, therefore, highlights one of those essential complications which characterize in the constitutional field the effort to work in the direction of organized international cooperation. At an experimental stage, such difficulties may be faced on a day-to-day basis, but in the long run they are likely to require imaginative and constructive constitutional innovations.

Perhaps a future generation, which knows the outcome of our present efforts, will look at them with some irony. They will see where we fumbled and they will find it difficult to understand why we did not see the direction more clearly and work more consistently towards the target it indicates. So it will always be, but let us hope that they will not find any reason to criticize us because of a lack of that combination of steadfastness of purpose and flexibility of approach which alone can guarantee that the possibilities which we are exploring will have been tested to the full. Working at the edge of the development of human society is to work on the brink of the unknown. Much of what is done will one day prove to have been of little avail. That is no excuse for the failure to act in accordance with our best understanding, in recognition of its limits but with faith in the ultimate result of the creative evolution in which it is our privilege to cooperate.

A question not of a man but of an institution

Statement before the General Assembly in reply to Chairman Krushchev and others, 26 September 1960. The statement is concerned primarily with the responsibilities of his own office in relation to the USSR demand that he resign and be replaced by a three-man directorate or troika.

When I asked for the privilege of exercising my right of reply at this stage of the general debate, it was not because I wanted to use this opportunity to correct any factual mistakes or misrepresentations. That should be unnecessary in the light of the very full debates in the Security Council and at the very recent emergency special session...

My reason for taking the floor now is another one. I felt that, before the debate goes any further, it would be appropriate for me to make clear to the Assembly what, in my view, is and is not the problem before the Assembly in certain respects on which the Secretary-General has been addressed by some speakers.

In those respects the General Assembly is facing a question not of any specific actions but of the principles guiding United Nations activities. In those respects it is a question not of a man but of an institution.

Just one week ago the General Assembly adopted a resolution regarding the Congo operation. It did so after a thorough debate and a full presentation of facts. As that is the situation it may well be asked why those 80 same facts should now be brought out again in the Assembly as a basis for new and far-reaching conclusions, perhaps involving even a question of confidence.

The question before the General Assembly is no longer one of certain actions but one of the principles guiding them. Time and again the United Nations has had to face situations in which a wrong move might have tended to throw the weight of the Organization over in favour of this or that specific party in a conflict of a primarily domestic character. To permit that to happen is indeed to intervene in domestic affairs contrary to the letter and the spirit of the Charter.

To avoid doing so is to be true to the letter and spirit of the Charter, whatever disappointment it might cause those who might have thought that they could add to their political weight by drawing the United Nations over to their side.

This is, of course, the basic reason for the principle spelled out at the very first stage of the Congo operation, and approved by the Security Council, to the effect that the United Nations Force is not under the orders of a government requesting its assistance and cannot be permitted to become a party to any internal conflict, be it one in which the government is engaged or not. It is common experience that nothing, in the heat of emotion, is regarded as more partial by one who takes himself the position of a party than strict impartiality.

Further, as I have said, this is a question not of a man but of an institution. Use whatever words you like, independence, impartiality, objectivity – they all describe essential aspects of what, without exception, must be the attitude of the Secretary-General. Such an attitude, which has found its clear and decisive expression in 81

Article 100 of the Charter, may at any stage become an obstacle for those who work for certain political aims which would be better served or more easily achieved if the Secretary-General compromised with this attitude. But if he did, how gravely he would then betray the trust of all those for whom the strict maintenance of such an attitude is their best protection in the world-wide fight for power and influence. Thus, if the office of the Secretary-General becomes a stumbling block for anyone, be it an individual, a group or a government, because the incumbent stands by the basic principle which must guide his whole activity, and if, for that reason, he comes under criticism, such criticism strikes at the very office and the concepts on which it is based. I would rather see that office break on strict adherence to the principle of independence, impartiality and objectivity than drift on the basis of compromise. That is the choice daily facing the Secretary-General. It is also the choice now openly facing the General Assembly, both in substance and in form. I believe that all those whose interests are safe-guarded by the United Nations will realize that the choice is not one of the convenience of the moment but one which is decisive for the future, their future.

If no positive advice is forthcoming, I have no choice but to follow my own conviction

One last word. Sometimes one gets the impression that the Congo operation is looked at as being in the hands of the Secretary-General, as somehow distinct from the United Nations. No: this is your operation, gentlemen. And this is true whether you represent the African and

Asian member countries, which carry the main burden for the Force and for its Command, or speak and act for other parts of the world. There is nothing in the Charter which puts responsibility of this kind on the shoulders of the Secretary-General or makes him the independent master of such an operation. It was the Security Council which, without any dissenting vote, gave this mandate to the Secretary-General on 14 July. It was the Security Council which, on 22 July, commended his report on the principles that should be applied. It was the Security Council, on 9 August, which, again without any dissenting vote, confirmed the authority given to the Secretary-General. Again, just a week ago, the General Assembly, without any dissenting vote, requested the Secretary-General to continue to take vigorous action. Indeed, as I said, this is your operation, gentlemen. It is for you to indicate what you want to have done. As the agent of the Organization I am grateful for any positive advice, but if no such positive advice is forthcoming – as happened in the Security Council on 21 August, when my line of implementation had been challenged from outside – then I have no choice but to follow my own conviction, guided by the principles to which I have just referred.

**I shall remain in my post in the interests
of all those other nations. /.../ By resigning,
I would throw the Organization to the winds**

Statement to the General Assembly, 3 October 1960:

The Head of the Soviet Delegation to the General Assembly, this morning, in exercising his right of reply, said, among many other things, that the present Secretary-General has always been biased against the social-ist countries, that he has used the United Nations in support of the colonial Powers fighting the Congolese Government and Parliament in order to impose 'a new yoke on the Congo,' and finally, that if I, myself, and I quote, 'do not muster up enough courage to resign, so to say in a chivalrous manner, then the Soviet Union will draw the necessary conclusions from the obtained situation.' In support of this challenge the representative of the Soviet Union said that it is not proper for a man who has 'flouted elementary justice to hold such an important post as that of the Secretary-General'. And later on he found reason to say to the delegates of this session that they should not 'submit to the clamorous phrases pronounced here' by me 'in attempts to justify the bloody crimes perpetrated against the Congolese people'.

The General Assembly can rightly expect an immediate reply from my side to a statement so directly addressed to me and regarding a matter of such potential significance.

The Assembly has witnessed over the last weeks how historical truth is established; once an allegation has been repeated a few times, it is no longer an allegation, it is an established fact, even if no evidence has been brought out in order to support it. However, facts are facts, and the true facts are there for whosoever cares for truth. Those who invoke history will certainly be heard by history. And they will have to accept its verdict as it will be pronounced on the basis of the facts by men free of mind and firm in their conviction that only on a scrutiny of truth can a future of peace be built.

I have no reason to defend myself or my colleagues

against the accusations and judgments to which you have listened. Let me say only this, that *you*, all of you, are the judges. No single party can claim that authority. I am sure you will be guided by truth and justice. In particular, let those who know what the United Nations has done and is doing in the Congo, and those who are not pursuing aims proper only to themselves, pass judgment on our actions there. Let the countries who have liberated themselves in the last fifteen years speak for themselves.

I regret that the intervention to which I have found it necessary to reply has again tended to personalize an issue which, as I have said, in my view is not a question of a man but of an institution. The man does not count, the institution does. A weak or nonexistent executive would mean that the United Nations would no longer be able to serve as an effective instrument for active protection of the interests of those many Members who need such protection. The man holding the responsibility as chief executive should leave if he weakens the executive; he should stay if this is necessary for its maintenance. This, and only this, seems to me to be the substantive criterion that has to be applied.

I said the other day that I would not wish to continue to serve as Secretary-General one day longer than such continued service was, and was considered to be, in the best interest of the Organization. The statement this morning seems to indicate that the Soviet Union finds it impossible to work with the present Secretary-General. This may seem to provide a strong reason why I should resign. However, the Soviet Union has also made it clear that, if the present Secretary-General were to resign now, they would not wish to elect a new incumbent but insist on an arrangement which – and this is my firm conviction based on broad experience – would make it impossible to maintain an effective executive. By resigning, I would, therefore, at the present difficult and dangerous juncture throw the Organization to the winds. I have no right to do so because I have a responsibility to all those Member States for which the Organization is of decisive importance, a responsibility which overrides all other considerations.

It is not the Soviet Union or, indeed, any other big powers who need the United Nations for their protection; it is all the others. In this sense the Organization is first of all *their* Organization, and I deeply believe in the wisdom with which they will be able to use it and guide it. I shall remain in my post during the term of my office as a servant of the Organization in the interests of all those other nations, as long as *they* wish me to do so.

In this context the representative of the Soviet Union spoke of courage. It is very easy to resign; it is not so easy to stay on. It is very easy to bow to the wish of a big power. It is another matter to resist. As is well known to all members of this Assembly, I have done so before on many occasions and in many directions. If it is the wish of those nations who see in the Organization their best protection in the present world, I shall now do so again.

The United Nations tries to counter tendencies to make the Congo »a happy hunting ground« for national and international interests

In July 1960 the Secretary-General was requested by the Security Council to provide military assistance to the Central Government of the Republic of Congo. The aim was to protect life and property within the Congo, in danger after the breakdown of the national security system, so as to eliminate the reasons for the Belgian military intervention and thereby to reduce what internationally had to be regarded as a serious threat to peace and security.

In a statement before the Security Council on 7 December 1960, the Secretary-General expressed »the deepest worry at seeing the way in which this Organization is abused in words, and abused as an instrument for purposes contrary to the Charter«:

We have been accused of servility in relation to the West, of softness in relation to the East, of supporting this or that man in the Congo whom one group or another on the world scene has chosen to make its symbol.

On February 15, 1961, Hammarskjöld stated before the Security Council:

For seven or eight months, through efforts far beyond the imagination of those who founded this Organization, it has tried to counter tendencies to introduce the big power conflict into Africa and put the young African countries under the shadow of the Cold War. It has done so with great risks and against heavy odds. It has done so at the cost of very great personal sacrifices for a great number of people. In the beginning the effort was successful, and I do not now hesitate to say that on more than one occasion the drift into a war with foreign power intervention of the Korean or Spanish type was avoided only thanks to the work done by the Organization, basing itself on African solidarity. We countered effectively efforts from all sides to make the Congo a happy hunting ground for national interests. To be a road-block to such efforts is to make yourself the target of attacks from all those who find their plans thwarted. 87

Is the Secretary-General – without instructions – legally and morally free to take no action in a matter considered to affect international peace and security?

Hammarskjöld referred to the dilemmas posed for the Secretary-General in a lecture delivered at Oxford University, 30 May 1961. Extract from the lecture:

These recent examples [the UN operations in Egypt after the Suez crisis 1956 and in Congo] demonstrate the extent to which the Member States have entrusted the Secretary-General with tasks that have required him to take action which unavoidably may have to run counter to the views of at least some of these Member States. The agreement reached in the general terms of a resolution, as we have seen, no longer need apply when more specific issues are presented. Even when the original resolution is fairly precise, subsequent developments, previously unforeseen, may render highly controversial the action called for under the resolution. Thus, for example, the unanimous resolution authorizing assistance to the Central Government of the Congo offered little guidance to the Secretary-General when that Government split into competing centers of authority, each claiming to be the Central Government and each supported by different groups of Member States within and outside the Security Council.

A simple solution for the dilemmas thus posed for the Secretary-General might seem to be for him to refer the problem to the political organ for it to resolve the question. Under a national parliamentary regime, this would often be the obvious course of action for the executive to take. Indeed, this is what the Secretary-General must also do whenever it is feasible. But the serious problems arise precisely because it is so often not possible for the organs themselves to resolve the controversial issue faced by the Secretary-General. When brought down to specific cases involving a clash of interests and positions, the required majority in the Security Council or General Assembly may not be available for any particular solution. This will frequently be evident in advance of a meeting and the Member States will conclude that it would be futile for the organs to attempt to reach a decision and consequently that the problem has to be left to the Secretary-General to solve on one basis or another, on his own risk but with as faithful an interpretation of the instructions, rights and obligations of the Organization as possible in view of international law and the decisions already taken.

It might be said that in this situation the Secretary-General should refuse to implement the resolution, since implementation would offend one or another group of Member States and open him to the charge that he has abandoned the political neutrality and impartiality essential to his office. The only way to avoid such criticism, it is said, is for the Secretary-General to refrain from execution of the original resolution until the organs have decided the issue by the required majority (and, in the case of the Security Council, with the unanimous concurrence of the permanent members) or he, maybe, has found another way to pass responsibility on to governments.

For the Secretary-General this course of action – or more precisely, non-action – may be tempting; it enables him to avoid criticism by refusing to act until other political organs resolve the dilemma. An easy refuge may thus appear to be available. But would such refuge be compatible with the responsibility placed upon the Secretary-General by the Charter? Is he entitled to refuse to carry out the decision properly reached by the organs, on the ground that the specific implementation would be opposed to positions some Member States might wish to take, as indicated, perhaps, by an earlier minority vote? Of course the political organs may always instruct him to discontinue the implementation of a resolution, but when they do not so instruct him and the resolution remains in effect, is the Secretary-General legally and morally free to take no action, particularly in a matter considered to affect international peace and security? Should he, for example, have abandoned the operation in the Congo because almost any decision he made as to the composition of the Force or its role would have been contrary to the attitudes of some Members as reflected in debates, and maybe even in votes, although not in decisions?

It is possible for the Secretary-General to carry out his tasks in controversial political situations with full regard to his exclusively international obligation under the Charter and without subservience to a particular national or ideological attitude

The answers seem clear enough in law; the responsibilities of the Secretary-General under the Charter cannot be laid aside merely because the execution of decisions by him is likely to be politically controversial. The Secretary-General remains under the obligation to carry out the policies as adopted by the organs; the essential 90 requirement is that he does this on the basis of his exclusively international responsibility and not in the interest of any particular State or groups of States.

This presents us with the crucial issue; is it possible for the Secretary-General to resolve controversial questions on a truly international basis without obtaining the formal decision of the organs? In my opinion and on the basis of my experience, the answer is in the affirmative; it is possible for the Secretary-General to carry out his tasks in controversial political situations with full regard to his exclusively international obligation under the Charter and without subservience to a particular national or ideological attitude.

The Secretary-General is not a delphic oracle who alone speaks for the international community

This is not to say that the Secretary-General is a kind of delphic oracle who alone speaks for the international community. He has available for his task varied means and resources.

Of primary importance in this respect are the principles and purposes of the Charter which are the fundamental law accepted by and binding on all States. Necessarily general and comprehensive, these principles and purposes still are specific enough to have practical significance in concrete cases.

The principles of the Charter are, moreover, supplemented by the body of legal doctrine and precepts that have been accepted by States generally, and particularly as manifested in the resolutions of United Nations organs. In this body of law there are rules and precedents that appropriately furnish guidance to the Secretary-

General when he is faced with the duty of applying a general mandate in circumstances that had not been envisaged by the resolution.

Considerations of principle and law, important as they are, do not of course suffice to settle all the questions posed by the political tasks entrusted to the Secretary-General Problems of political judgment still remain. In regard to these problems, the Secretary-General must find constitutional means and techniques to assist him, insofar as possible, in reducing the element of purely personal judgment. In my experience I have found several arrangements of value to enable the Secretary-General to obtain what might be regarded as the representative opinion of the Organization in respect of the political issues faced by him.

One such arrangement might be described as the institution of the permanent missions to the United Nations, through which the Member States have enabled the Secretary-General to carry on frequent consultations safeguarded by diplomatic privacy.

Another arrangement, which represents a further development of the first, has been the advisory committees of the Secretary-General, such as those on UNEF and the Congo, composed of representatives of governments most directly concerned with the activity involved, and also representing diverse political positions and interests. These advisory committees have furnished a large measure of the guidance required by the Secretary-General in carrying out his mandates relating to UNEF and the Congo operations. They have provided an essential link between the judgment of the executive and the consensus of the political bodies.

Neutral and neutrality

The Secretary-General may refuse to indicate a stand in emerging conflicts in order thus to preserve the neutrality of the office – or accord himself the right to take a stand in these conflicts to the extent that such stands can be firmly based on the Charter and its principles

From address to Students Association, Copenhagen, 2 May 1959:

Here the office I represent enters the picture. The Secretary-General is elected by the General Assembly, but on the recommendation of the Security Council, and this recommendation requires unanimity among the five permanent Council members. The purpose of this arrangement is to ensure that the Secretary-General shall, as far as possible, be placed outside or lifted above conflicts which may split the Assembly or the Council. From another point of view, the rules of election aim at ensuring that the Secretary-General, as one of the main organs of the United Nations, shall have the opportunity of functioning as the spokesman of the Organization in its capacity as an independent opinion factor. This desire is natural and not particularly difficult to satisfy concerning administrative questions, which of course should be insulated as far as possible from all political conflicts. The problem is pointed up when the political and diplomatic responsibilities of the Secretary-General come into play.

There are two possible lines of action for the Secretary-General in the political questions falling within the competence of the Organization, two lines which have both had their advocates in the debate about the office. The Secretary-General may interpret his constitutionally objective position in such a way as to refuse to indicate a stand in emerging conflicts in order thus to preserve the neutrality of the office. He may, however, also accord himself the right to take a stand in these conflicts to the extent that such stands can be firmly based on the Charter and its principles and thus express what may be called the independent judgment of the Organization.

It goes without saying that, to the extent that the Secretary-General follows this latter course, his office assumes an importance quite different from what happens if he chooses what one might call negative neutrality as his leading principle. If the Secretary-General represents an independent but positive evaluation, free of partisan influences and determined by the purposes of the Charter, this means not only that he reinforces the weight that independent opinion may come to carry in the negotiations. Step by step, he thereby also builds up a practice which may open the door to a more generally recognized independent influence for the Organization as such in the political evolution.

**An independant political and diplomatic activity
of the Secretary-General as the »neutral« representative
of the United Nations**

The difficulty of a policy along these latter lines is obvious. A positive influence, politically, for the Secretary-

General can be imagined in practice only on two conditions. First, he must have the full confidence of the Member States, at least as to his independence and his freedom from personal motives. Second, he must accept the limitation of acting mainly on inner lines without publicity. In nine cases out of ten, a Secretary-General would destroy his chances of exerting an independent influence on developments by publicly appealing to opinion over the heads of the governments. Only in rare exceptions – in the tenth case, one might say – is this what the situation requires, and then he must of course be prepared to see his future value as a negotiator endangered or even lost. In the latter case, he ought, naturally, to resign from his post.

Sometimes, it has proved difficult to gain understanding of the fact that the independent influence of the Secretary-General largely is indirectly proportionate to his degree of discretion. Cases such as the Suez and Hungary crises, when on the basis of the Charter he took a direct political stand in public, have been considered instances of what he ought to do more often. Everybody is free to judge for himself. What I have just said reflects my own experience and the conclusions I have reached.

To the extent that events have led the governments to accord an independent position as spokesman of the United Nations to the Secretary-General even politically, this has also given him wider opportunities for independent diplomatic activity. One instance during this year may be mentioned. On the basis of an invitation from two Member States, the Secretary-General recently sent a personal representative on a good offices mission to these countries.* This was a measure of a kind that used to be taken exclusively by the Security Council. In this case it was taken without a decision by the Security Council, after the Secretary-General had informed the Council of his intentions in order to give its members an opportunity to raise objections if they so desired.

This action, which may lead to the development of a new pattern – other governments have made two or three proposals of a similar nature – is an example of what I should like to call active preventive diplomacy, which may be conducted by the United Nations, through the Secretary-General or in other forms, in many situations where no government or group of governments and no regional organization would be able to act in the same way. That such interventions are possible for the United Nations is explained by the fact that in the manner I have indicated, the Organization has begun to gain a certain independent position, and that this tendency has led to the acceptance of an independent political and diplomatic activity on the part of the Secretary-General as the 'neutral' representative of the Organization.

*Cambodia and Thailand had broken diplomatic relations. These were restored as the result of the good offices exercised by the Secretary-General's personal representative, Ambassador Johan Beck-Friis of Sweden.

Are there neutral men?

From lecture at Oxford University, 30 May 1961:

In a recent article Mr. Walter Lippmann tells about an interview in Moscow with Mr. Krushchev. According to the article, Chairman Krushchev stated that 'while there are neutral countries, there are no neutral men,' and the author draws the conclusion that it is now the view of the Soviet Government 'that there can be no such thing as an impartial civil servant in this deeply divided world, and that the kind of political celibacy which the British theory of the civil servant calls for, is in international affairs a fiction.'

Whether this accurately sums up the views held by the Soviet Government, as reflected in the interview, or not, one thing is certain: The attitude which the article reflects is one which we find nowadays in many political quarters, communist and non-communist alike, and it raises a problem which cannot be treated lightly. In fact, it challenges basic tenets in the philosophy of both the League of Nations and the United Nations, as one of the essential points on which these experiments in international cooperation represent an advance beyond traditional 'conference diplomacy' is the introduction on the international arena of joint permanent organs, employing a neutral civil service, and the use of such organs for executive purposes on behalf of all the members of the organizations. Were it to be considered that the experience shows that this radical innovation in international life rests on a false assumption, because 'no man can be neutral,' then we would be thrown back to 1919, and a searching re-appraisal would become necessary.

The Charter gives to the Secretary-General an explicit political role

It has substantial significance in the Charter, for it entitles the General Assembly and the Security Council to 97 entrust the Secretary-General with tasks involving the execution of political decisions, even when this would bring him – and with him the Secretariat and its members – into the arena of possible political conflict. The organs are, of course, not required to delegate such tasks to the Secretary-General but it is clear that they *may* do so. Moreover, it may be said that in doing so the General Assembly and the Security Council are in no way in conflict with the spirit of the Charter – even if some might like to give the word 'chief administrative officer' in Article 97 a normative and limitative significance – since the Charter itself gives to the Secretary-General an explicit political role.

It is Article 99 more than any other which was considered by the drafters of the Charter to have transformed the Secretary-General of the United Nations from a purely administrative official to one with an explicit political responsibility.

Legal scholars have observed that Article 99 not only confers upon the Secretary-General a right to bring matters to the attention of the Security Council but that this right carries with it, by necessary implication, a broad discretion to conduct inquiries and to engage in informal diplomatic activity in regard to matters which 'may threaten the maintenance of international peace and security.' /.../

If a demand for neutrality is made, by present critics of the international civil service, with the intent that the international civil servant should not be permitted to take a stand on political issues, in response to requests of the General Assembly or the Security Council, then the demand is in conflict with the Charter itself. If, however, 'neutrality' means that the international civil servant, also in executive tasks with political implications, must remain wholly uninfluenced by national or group interests or ideologies, then the obligation to observe such neutrality is just as basic to the Charter concept of the international civil service as it was to the concept once found in the Covenant of the League. Due to the circumstances then prevailing the distinction to which I have just drawn attention probably was never clearly made in the League, but it has become fundamental for the interpretation of the actions of the Secretariat as established by the Charter.

If integrity drives the international civil servant into positions of conflict with this or that interest, then that conflict is a sign of his neutrality

Experience has thus indicated that the international civil servant may take steps to reduce the sphere within which he has to take stands on politically controversial issues. In summary, it may be said that he will carefully seek guidance in the decisions of the main organs, in statements relevant for the interpretation of those decisions, in the Charter and in generally recognized principles of law, remembering that by his actions he may set important precedents. Further, he will submit as complete reporting to the main organs as circumstances permit, seeking their guidance whenever such guidance seems to be possible to obtain. Even if all of these steps are taken, it will still remain, as has been amply demonstrated in practice, that the reduced area of discretion will be large enough to expose the international Secretariat to heated political controversy and to accusations of a lack of neutrality.

I have already drawn attention to the ambiguity of the word 'neutrality' in such a context. It is obvious from what I have said that the international civil servant cannot be accused of lack of neutrality simply for taking a stand on a controversial issue when this is his duty and cannot be avoided. But there remains a serious intellectual and moral problem as we move within an area inside which personal judgment must come into play. Finally, we have to deal here with a question of integrity or with, if you please, a question of conscience.

The international civil servant must keep himself under the strictest observation. He is not requested to be a neuter in the sense that he has to have no sympathies or antipathies, that there are to be no interests which are close to him in his personal capacity or that he is to have no ideas or ideals that matter for him. However, he is requested to be fully aware of those human reactions and meticulously check himself so that they are not permitted to influence his actions. This is nothing unique. Is not every judge professionally under the same obligation?

If the international civil servant knows himself to be free from such personal influences in his actions and guided solely by the common aims and rules laid down for, and by the Organization he serves and by recognized legal principles, then he has done his duty, and then he can face the criticism which, even so, will be unavoidable. As I said, at the final last, this is a question of integrity, and if integrity in the sense of respect for law and respect for truth were to drive him into positions of conflict with this or that interest, then that conflict is a sign of his neutrality and not of his failure to observe neutrality – then it is in line, not in conflict, with his duties as an international civil servant.

In a very deep, human sense there is no neutral individual but there is neutral action by the right kind of man

From transcript of press conference 12 June 1961 with comments on the Oxford lecture:

It may be true that in a very deep, human sense there is no neutral individual, because, as I said at Oxford, everyone, if he is worth anything, has to have his ideas and ideals – things which are dear to him, and so on. But what I do claim is that even a man who is in that sense not neutral can very well undertake and carry through neutral actions, because that is an act of integrity. That is to say, I would say there is no neutral man, but there is, if you have integrity, neutral action by the right kind of man. And 'neutrality' may develop, after all, into a kind of *jeu de mots*. I am not a neutral as regards the Charter; I am not neutral as regards facts. But that is not what we mean. What is meant by 'neutrality' in this kind of debate, is of course, neutrality in relation to interests; and there I do claim that there is no insurmountable difficulty for anybody with the proper kind of guiding principles in carrying through such neutrality one hundred per cent.

The diplomat and public opinion

The most important new factor in diplomacy: mass public opinion as a living force in international affairs

From address to Foreign Policy Association, New York, 21 October 1953:

His [the diplomat's] relationship to his own people has also changed. This has come as a fruit of broader education, of a development of the democratic system and of the revolutionary growth of the mass media of communication. The diplomat may still confer behind closed doors, but he will be met by reporters and photographers when he comes out. His words will reach everybody by press and film and radio and television. His personality will be known to vast numbers for whom in other times he would have been only a name, or less than a name.

These last considerations lead me on to the final, least tangible, but perhaps most important new factor in diplomacy: mass public opinion as a living force in international affairs. Of course, this public opinion has as its background the new mass media of communication, but as a psychological phenomenon and a political factor it is not sufficiently explained by this background. It is the expression of a democratic mass civilization that is still in its infancy, giving to the man in the street and to group reactions a new significance in foreign policy.

Is it possible to envisage the making of foreign policy

and the tasks and techniques of diplomacy in the same way for a situation such as the one just described as for previous stages in history? The reply must be *no*. The diplomat who works bilaterally on a national basis without the widest perspective, without recognition – and a proper handling – of the publicity aspect of his work, or without giving to public opinion its proper place in the picture, has little place in our world of today.

The United Nations operates in a glass house – and it should operate in a glass house in order to serve its purposes

From address to Foreign Policy Association, New York, 21 October 1953:

A characteristic of the new diplomacy, developing on the multilateral basis or with multilateral aims, is that it has to operate in daylight to an extent unknown in the diplomacy of a traditional type. The importance of publicity for good and for bad in international diplomacy may be studied with the greatest profit in the international organizations. It has been said that one should never forget that the United Nations operates in a glass house. I would add that in our world of today it could not operate properly under any other conditions; in fact, in my view, it should operate in a glass house in order to serve its purposes. Multilateral diplomacy is by its very nature such that the old secrecy has lost its place and justification.

But there should be no mistakes. Publicity is right and necessary in multilateral diplomacy. However, it also represents a danger. Open diplomacy may, as a prominent delegate to the United Nations recently pointed out, easily become frozen diplomacy. This comes about when open diplomacy is turned into diplomacy by public statements made merely to satisfy segments of domestic public opinion or to gain some propaganda advantage elsewhere.

Considerations of national prestige also enter into the picture. Legislators and members of parliaments in our democracies have long been used to the give and take of debate on state and national issues, to the compromises that are fashioned every day in the legislative process, to accepting defeat as well as victory in voting as part of the normal course of politics. Neither the diplomats who practice multilateral diplomacy on the public stage nor the governments they represent are yet fully acclimated to this new aspect of international relations. Nor, it must be said, is public opinion itself. Too often, any modification of national positions once taken publicly, or acceptance of sensible compromise, is shunned out of fear that it will be labelled appeasement or defeat.

It is part of the diplomat's responsibility to help and to lead public opinion

It may seem to him that this opinion, being more or less the master of his masters, is the most important single factor in his planning of the implementation of international policy. And, of course, it is a factor of singular importance. No diplomat can depart too far from what is accepted or acceptable to public opinion in those quarters which give weight to his arguments. But it does not follow from this that he should simply let himself be guided by anticipated reactions of the public. A diplomacy that gives full weight to recognized or anticipated public opinion may in a decisive way also give direction to this opinion.

In the modern world of mass media and publicity no diplomat trying to respond to the demands of the situations can be only a servant. He must to some extent and in some respects also be a leader by looking beyond the immediate future and going underneath the superficial reactions, be they expressed by ever so powerful news organs catering for what are believed to be the wishes of the broad masses – wishes which may in reality be as loosely attached to the man in the street as the suits which he decides to wear this year. It is part of the diplomat's responsibility not only to lead public opinion towards acceptance of the lasting consequences of the interdependence of our world. He must also help public opinion to become as accustomed to the necessity for give and take and for compromise in international politics as it has long been on questions of state and local concern.

No diplomat will adjust himself to the new type of publicity – which is unavoidable in all official activities but is of special importance in multilateral diplomacy – unless he has the courage of his own actions. No diplomat is likely to meet the demands of public opinion on him as a representative in international policy unless he understands this opinion and unless he respects it deeply enough to give it leadership when he feels that the opinion does not truly represent the deeper and finally decisive aspirations in the minds and hearts of the people.

The ultimate test of a diplomacy adequate to our world is its capacity to evoke this kind of response from the people and thus to rally public opinion behind what is wise and necessary for the peace and progress of the world.

Leadership

**The Secretary-General has to try out
and reach the minds and hearts of people**

From address to American Political Science Association, Washington, 11 September 1953:

The Secretary-General – and I use him as a symbol for all of the Secretariat – is facing a public relations problem of a delicate and difficult nature. He is not out to 'sell' anything. His is not a propaganda operation. But he has to try and reach the minds and hearts of people so as to get the United Nations' efforts firmly based in public reaction. As I said, we are not selling anything, but we feel that what we are doing is something that should have the support of the simple reactions of plain men, if we manage to tell them our story in the right way. So, the question of public relations to the Secretary-General develops into a question of human relations.

The United Nations has to activate in its support people's urge to live together and work together in peace and decency. For that reason the United Nations has to try to create a new awareness of human and national interdependence. In order to be able to do so it will have to understand what makes so difficult the development of such an awareness. It will have to understand – and challenge – the fear that motivates so much of human action, the fear that is our worst enemy but which, somehow, seems to taint at least some corner of the heart of every man.

So the Secretary-General of the United Nations is led into very wide fields which are under the reign of political science. In his efforts he may have to enter the world of 'An American Dilemma' (Gunnar Myrdal) and the land of 'The Lonely Crowd', (David Riesman) and he must give such knowledge its proper background in the broodings of the de Tocquevilles and Schumpeters.

The ultimate challenge is whether man shall master his world or let himself be mastered by it

When tackling the question of interdependence the United Nations must try and analyze for itself what determines group relations of the kind which international political history so often mirrors. I have already mentioned the element of fear but there are other factors. We would be misled if we thought about international relations only in terms of diplomatic history. Economic policies and power politics are other forces doing their work in the background. We move here in the shadow of Burckhardt. We have to listen to those who analyze the dynamics of the great population movements and the national revivals. Finally we may arrive at a point where we have to analyze the situation with the finest tools of political economy in order to see how material factors determine or clash with human reactions.

You may feel that my departure from the beaten path has led me very far indeed, when I try to cover in one sweeping movement spheres studied by the theoretical economist, the historian and the student of the human mind. However, all the parts of political and social science are linked together. The man mastering all the various aspects does not exist. But each of us may be able to make a contribution and so to build up a picture which, although far from complete, gives us a rough map of the waters that we have to sail.

The ultimate challenge to the political sciences – and to us all – is whether man shall master his world and his history or let himself be mastered by a world and a history which after all is made by man. There cannot be more than one reply to this question. Man must master his world, but in order to do so, he must know it.

The peoples are eagerly and anxiously expecting leadership to bring them out of the present nightmare

From statement on the arms race before the Security Council, 29 April 1958:

On a previous occasion I have stated as my opinion, that the Secretary-General has not only the right but the duty to intervene when he feels that he should do so in support of the purposes of this Organization and the principles laid down in the Charter. He cannot assume for himself the right to 'speak for man' but he must subordinate himself to his duty to express the significance of the aspirations of man, as set out in the Charter, for problems before this Council or the General Assembly.

As a reason for the stalemate in the field of disarmament, Hammarskjöld states:

Still another reason and, of course, the basic one, is the crisis of trust from which all mankind is suffering at the present juncture and which is reflected in an unwillingness to take any moves in a positive direction at their face value and a tendency to hold back a positive response because of a fear of being misled.

Each government is in close contact with the opinion of the man in the street in its own country. For that reason, I am sure that all governments are in a position to confirm my statement that the peoples are eagerly and anxiously expecting leadership to bring them out of the present nightmare. The government taking a fruitful initiative will be hailed as a benefactor by the peoples. The governments responding in a positive spirit so as to give effect to such an attempt to turn the development, will share the merit with the one who took the first step.

I have felt it incumbent on me to state these few simple reactions. I have done so under my obligations to the peoples whose voice is reflected in the Charter under which I am acting. I trust that my intervention will not be misinterpreted as a taking of sides, but merely as an expression of profound feelings which are current all over the world and which have a right to be heard here also outside the framework of government policies.

I hope that each one of the governments, represented around this table, will wish to try out the line of trust as a way out of the disintegration and decline under which we now all suffer.

Leadership must be substituted for power

From address at University of Lund, Sweden, 4 May 1959:

It means that leadership is substituted for power – leadership both in giving other peoples their chance and in assisting them, without issuing commands, to find the best way to develop their spiritual and material resources.

On a modest level and to an all-too-small extent, the Organization I represent is working in the direction I have indicated. It is based on a philosophy of solidarity. It attempts to convey to the less favoured nations, in the first place, knowledge, but also material resources which will give them the chance for a development and position corresponding to their potentialities. It tries to find forms in which the ancient nations which are now gaining or have gained their freedom, may find their new place without frictions. It accords them all an equal voice in the councils, independent of race, history and physical or economic power. The latter respect is one in which, in particular, one encounters a skepticism similar in nature to that which once formed an obstacle to universal suffrage. One may be conscious of the hazards of such an experiment and yet be convinced that it is necessary and has to be carried out. In this case, the experiment must succeed. To achieve this, those who work for the new synthesis must not deny or question the principles on which it must be based.

To an increasing extent, experts from the West have gone out to the new nations in Asia and Africa to help the governments in different posts. In this, they have embarked on a career entirely in the spirit of the age, and one which belongs to the future. I hope that from Sweden, and indeed from this university, men and women will go out into the world in the various forms which are available, not as some kind of missionaries either for the West or for a world community, but in order to serve, by practical work, the evolution towards the synthesis which is on the way.

They can do it, aware of the riches of the cultural heritage which is theirs and of all that Europe stands for, but they should do it in awareness, also, that the best and soundest way to perpetuate this cultural heritage is to meet other peoples and other cultures in humble respect for the unique gifts that they, in turn, have offered and still offer to humanity.

They should realize that it is a sign of the highest culture to be really capable of listening, learning and therefore also responding in a way which helps the less favoured ones; while it is a privilege reserved for the half-educated who is unaware of his limitations to be a poor listener in a feeling of his own false superiority. Leadership – the word I have used to designate what may come instead of superior power – is a dangerous word if one does not keep in mind that the most influential leaders in the European cultural evolution were askers of questions like Socrates or the carpenter's son from Nazareth.

An increasing number of nations look to the United Nations for leadership

From Introduction to the Annual Report 1959–1960:

The United Nations has increasingly become the main platform – and the main protector of the interests – of those many nations who feel themselves strong as members of the international family but who are weak in isolation. Thus, an increasing number of nations have
come to look to the United Nations for leadership and

support in ways somewhat different from those natural in the light of traditional international diplomacy. They look to the Organization as a spokesman and as an agent for principles which give them strength in an international concert in which other voices can mobilize all the weight of armed force, wealth, an historical role and that influence which is the other side of a special responsibility for peace and security. Therefore, a weakening of the Organization, resulting from an attempt to achieve results at the cost of principles, is a loss not only for the future but also immediately in respect of the significance of the Organization for the vast majority of nations and in respect of their confidence in the Organization on which its strength in our present-day world ultimately depends.

There are in the Charter elements of a thinking which, I believe, belongs to an earlier period in the development of the world community. I have in mind especially the concept that the permanent members of the Security Council should not only, as is natural, be recognized as carrying special responsibility for peace and security, but that, further, these permanent members, working together, should represent a kind of 'built-in' directing group for the world community as organized in the United Nations.

The fifteen years which have passed since the founding of the United Nations have witnessed a different development. In the first place, we have seen a split among the permanent members which, in fact, has created the major war risk of today and considerably hampered the development of the Organization. But, further, we have experienced a growth into independence of a majority of States of two great continents, with other interests, other traditions and other concepts of international politics than those of the countries of Europe and the Americas. Who can deny that today the countries of Asia or the countries of Africa, acting in a common spirit, represent powerful elements in the international community, in their ways as important as any of the big Powers, although lacking in their military and economic potential?

The United Nations is an organic creation of the political situation facing our generation. At the same time, however, the international community has, so to say, come to political self-consciousness in the Organization and, therefore, can use it in a meaningful way in order to influence those very circumstances of which the Organization is a creation.

The United Nations Charter

All men and women of good will can influence the course of history in the direction of the ideals expressed in the Charter

From address to American Association for the United Nations, New York, 14 September 1953:

As you all know, the United Nations Charter is based on what I may call a working hypothesis. This is that all the great nations and groups of nations must belong to it if it is to succeed. The Charter does not quite say that membership should be universal, but that is its spirit.

We know that this hypothesis is being challenged, and challenged not only by those who do not yet fully understand and accept the essential interdependency of our world today, but also by truly internationally minded people animated by the most serious desire to build a better world. Yet it seems to me that the idea of the United Nations as a club to which only the like-minded will be admitted, in which membership is a privilege and expulsion is the retribution for wrong-doing, is totally unrealistic and self-defeating.

Look anywhere in the world today. Is there any solution in sight except peacefully negotiated agreements? Granted that at a given moment the prospects for such agreements seem dim indeed. What is the alternative? Only the attempt to establish 'one world' by force of arms. And that is no alternative. Such an attempt would lead to a catastrophe just as fatal to the presumed victor, as to the vanquished. Beyond that, history and social conditions have given us a world so heterogeneous that the conditions simply do not exist for a one world established by force. I believe this should be recognized as true no matter on what ideology you base your judgment and for whatever way of life you plead.

I think that such a view of the United Nations as I have outlined will help all of us who are working for its success, whether as citizens or officials, in judging wisely each issue as it comes along and in meeting the various currents of criticism and opposition. No state, no group of states, no world organization, can grip the world and shape it, neither by force, nor by any formula of words in a charter or a treaty. There are no absolute answers to the agonies and searchings of our time. But all men and women of good will can influence the course of history in the direction of the ideals expressed in the Charter.

Recognition of the principle of self-determination of peoples means that democratic ideals are given a world-wide application

From Introduction to the Annual Report 1955–1956:

Article I of the United Nations Charter states that one of the main purposes of the United Nations is 'to develop friendly relations among nations based on respect for the principle of equal rights and self-determination of peoples.' This recognition of the principle of self-determination as a basis for friendly relations among nations means that democratic ideals, which have carried many
peoples to new heights, are given a world-wide applica-

tion. The governments signatories to the Charter have formulated here a policy which, in the light of history, may well come to be regarded as one of the most significant landmarks of our times.

The United Nations, of course, is not the cause of the great change through which more than half of mankind, for centuries voiceless, has grown into or is now moving towards membership of the world community as citizens of independent national States. But the Organization is inevitably a focal point for the efforts so to guide the difficult and delicate development that this progress may be achieved in peace and become a means to reinforce peace.

To say this is not to overlook that, in many cases, other procedures than those created by the Charter may provide possibilities of working out fundamental elements of the new relationship. The Charter itself foresees negotiations between parties as an initial step in the solution of conflicts which are unavoidable during a period of fundamental change. But I believe that such negotiations gain by being conducted against the background of the purposes and principles of the Charter and that the results can usefully be brought within the framework of the United Nations. If the negotiations prove unsuccessful, they should then be followed up on the basis laid down and in the forms prescribed by the Charter.

It is important to remember that the Charter endorses self-determination as a basis for friendly relations among nations. Both unrealistic impatience in the movement towards self-determination and wasteful resistance to it would contradict this philosophy of the Charter by leading to conflicts which might threaten peace. Under the Charter, the nations concerned are therefore called upon to further the movement toward self-determination in such a manner as to strengthen the bonds of world community instead of weakening them.

Forces that stimulate this movement have also led to the emergence of a new nationalism. This nationalism can be a constructive element, raising the dignity and stature of peoples and mobilizing their best moral resources. But, in a period of severe emotional strains, it may also find expressions which are in fact hostile to the steady growth of the very national life it aims to serve. The United Nations may help in avoiding such a self-defeating development.

The aims which the principles of the Charter are to safeguard are holier than the policies of any single nation or people

From statement before the Security Council, 31 October 1956, since British and French forces had begun landings in the Suez Canal zone:

This afternoon I wish to make the following declaration: The principles of the Charter are, by far, greater than the Organization in which they are embodied, and the aims which they are to safeguard are holier than the policies of any single nation or people. As a servant of the Organization, the Secretary-General has the duty to maintain his usefulness by avoiding public stands on conflicts between Member nations unless and until such an action might help to resolve the conflict. However, the discretion and impartiality thus imposed on the Secretary-General by the character of his immediate task,

may not degenerate into a policy of expediency. He must also be a servant of the principles of the Charter, and its aims must ultimately determine what for him is right and wrong. For that he must stand. A Secretary-General cannot serve on any other assumption than that – within the necessary limits of human frailty and honest differences of opinion – all Member nations honor their pledge to observe all articles of the Charter. He should also be able to assume that those organs which are charged with the task of upholding the Charter, will be in a position to fulfill their task.

The bearing of what I have just said must be obvious to all without any elaboration from my side. Were the Members to consider that another view of the duties of the Secretary-General than the one here stated would better serve the interests of the Organization, it is their obvious right to act accordingly.

In the course of the meeting the representatives of the Great Powers including France, the United Kingdom and the USSR as well as the United States and other members indicated their acceptance of this statement of the right and duty of the Secretary-General to speak and act in support of the principles of the Charter in such circumstances.

A similar statement on the duties of the Secretary General and his understanding of the stands he has to take was made by Hammarskjöld on 4 november 1956 after the attacks by Soviet troops in Hungary.

**I doubt whether it would be really desirable
to abolish the veto**

From address to Indian Council of World Affairs, New Delhi, 3 February 1956:

It has been, especially during the discussions of the revision of the Charter that the question of the veto, the privileged voting position of the permanent members of the Security Council, has come up for discussion again and again. Harsh words have been said about the use or abuse of the veto; sometimes there seems to me to be a tendency to underestimate the difficulties for the countries possessing the veto right to maintain their line of action in the Council in a way that is faithful to their opinions, without having recourse to the veto. However, the practical question is: Is there any reason to do away with the veto, is there any possibility even to do away with it? I think everybody is agreed that at present the veto could not be abolished, and I doubt whether it would be really desirable to abolish the veto. We must not forget that the veto, from the point of view of those countries which are not permanent members of the Security Council, is a guarantee that decisions taken by the Security Council are unanimous as among the permanent members. Some of the functions of the Security Council involve very heavy responsibilities for all Members of the United Nations, very heavy responsibilities in the military field, in the field of sanctions, police actions and so on. It should not be forgotten that for those countries whose hands would be tied by a decision of the Security Council, it does mean something that there is unanimity of the permanent members behind the decision.

So far as the practical possibility of getting rid of the veto is concerned, I should like here to quote Mr. Krishna Menon who, I think, was the one who coined the phrase: »The day we can get rid of the veto there is no reason to get rid of it.« This is quite true. The very day we can reach unanimity on the abolition of the veto, we have reached a state of understanding among the permanent members of the Security Council which certainly would mean that the veto would no longer be a major obstacle to action by the Security Council.

Military force

**The Charter permits defensive alliances but
the United Nations' military force aims at a universal
system for the maintenance of peace**

From address to Students Association, Copenhagen, 2 May 1959:

Chapter VII of the United Nations Charter authorizes,
in certain circumstances, the Security Council to use
military force to maintain peace. It is important to realize what this means. This is not collective security of a
kind which a defensive alliance can provide. The Charter expressly permits the formation of such alliances,
but the United Nations itself is something else again.
The possibilities of the Organization to use military
force are limited to acts of coercion in the name of the
world community against a nation which violates the
peace. Such an action requires unanimity of the Great
Powers. This unanimity has a two-fold significance.
Without it a military police action lacks the foundation
necessary to be fully effective. And without it the United
Nations would also, in contrast to the fundamental idea
on which it is built, be capable of transformation into
an instrument of military force in a conflict between the
Great Powers – with all that this might mean for the
other Member States. The rule of unanimity in combination with the right to form defensive alliances defines
the position of the Organization. It has never been
meant as an organ of collective security of the alliance

type, but it is aimed at a universal system for the maintenance of peace which may have, as a natural complement, defensive alliances.

Whatever role may be accorded to defensive alliances, experience shows that there are essential tasks in maintenance of peace which fall and must fall outside their province

The instances I have recalled* – I might of course have named others – are interesting because they show how the United Nations may fill vital needs in maintaining peace by executive measures. In these respects there is at present no substitute and no alternative for the Organization. The tasks of this kind which it has assumed could not have been fulfilled outside the United Nations framework by any single country or group of countries. These are security needs in the widest sense, which can be met only on the basis of universality and neutrality in the sense of freedom from partisan interests. Whatever role may be accorded to defensive alliances and similar arrangements, experience shows that there are essential tasks in the maintenance of peace which fall, and must fall, entirely outside the province of such groupings.

*In Gaza the United Nations formed a police force in 1956, described as a quasi-military organ; in Lebanon an observation group 1958; in Jordan a civilian organization of a very limited size 1958.

A permanent United Nations force is not advisable – but UN arrangements for preparing military operations in emerging situations

From address to Members of Parliament, London, 2 April 1958:

The Force was created in an emergency situation, and for that reason we had to improvise. We had to improvise in the field of international law, in the field of military organization, in various fields where usually one does not really like to jump into cold water and start swimming without having learned how best to swim. That means that the Force, as established, cannot, in my view, serve as a good foundation on which to build anything permanent of the very same form. But it does serve as an extremely useful and valuable experiment. We have learned very much. And, in the Secretariat, I have started a study which will digest our experiences, work out some kind of blueprint, master texts of the kind needed for this kind of operation. That means that, if another operation of a similar type should arise, where the same need would be felt, we would not have the Force but we would have everything ready in such a way that we would not again improvise. We would not again make those unavoidable mistakes into which, so to speak, you rush when you just must get the thing going without having had the time to study it carefully before.

In a sense, what I have said here is a reply to the question of whether or not, at the present stage, we should work for a permanent Force. I think the counsel of wisdom is, in the first instance, to digest the experience, to work out what I call the blueprints, the master texts for agreements, for orders, and so on and so forth ... to get that firmly in hand, and then work with that as the emergency arrangement.

Those who are interested in the financial question may, I think, take special pleasure in the fact that this does not cost anything – and the other operation is an extremely costly one, as our experience has shown.

Advisable if governments would maintain a state of preparedness so as to be able to meet possible military demands from the United Nations

From Introduction to the Annual Report 1959–1960:

It should, however, be stressed that the Congo experience has strengthened my conviction that the organization of a standing United Nations force would represent an unnecessary and impractical measure, especially in view of the fact that every new situation and crisis which the Organization will have to face is likely to present new problems as to the best adjustment of the composition of a force, its equipment, its training and its organization.

It is an entirely different matter if governments, in a position and willing to do so, would maintain a state of preparedness so as to be able to meet possible demands from the United Nations. And it is also an entirely different matter, for the Organization itself, to have a state of preparedness with considerable flexibility and in the hands of a qualified staff which quickly and smoothly can adjust their plans to new situations and assist the Secretary-General in the crucially important first stages of the execution of a decision by the main organs to set up a United Nations force, whatever its type or task.

New diplomatic techniques

The nerve signals from a wound in the world are felt at once through the body of mankind

From address to Foreign Policy Association, New York, 21 October 1953:

Diplomacy as a professional activity is certainly one of the most ancient and conservative. There has always been a need for negotiation between nations and the techniques and psychology of such negotiations have, at least until recently, undergone no great changes through all the centuries. I guess that the emissaries of Egypt or Greece or Rome had to approach their problems in very much the same way as the emissaries of Napoleon's France, Bismarck's Germany and Queen Victoria's Great Britain.

However, I do not think that it is an exaggeration to say that the world with which modern diplomacy has to deal differs from the world of the nineteenth century in those respects which interest us here, more than the world of the nineteenth century differed from its predecessors.

But technological development has altered the basis for diplomatic action also in another respect which should be just as obvious to everybody but seems sometimes to be forgotten. Just as the diplomat of today must rule out war as an instrument of policy, so he must recognize that in the new state of interdependence between nations war anywhere becomes the concern of all. The intricate web of relationships which now exist have as part of their basis the new means of communication which have overnight made our world so much smaller than it was in previous generations. We are all very conscious of the fact that it is now but a question of hours for military forces to reach distant parts of the globe and that the old considerations of strategy based on geographic separation no longer count for much.

News also reaches us from all corners of the globe almost as quickly as if we had been eye-witnesses. We are parties to an action practically at the very moment it is undertaken. The nerve signals from a wound are felt at once all through the body of mankind.

My most challenging task is to develop all the potentialities of the unique diplomatic institution called the Secretary-General

From address to American Political Science Association, Washington, 11 September 1954:

Traditional diplomatic techniques are, of course, in principle bilateral. That is true even if many nations happen to be represented at the conference table. A truly multilateral approach to diplomacy does not come into being until an instrument is created which represents a denationalized platform for negotiations or a denationalized instrument for a number of governments. In the Annual Report to the Eighth Assembly I have said that I believe we have only begun to explore the full potentialities of the United Nations as an instrument for multilateral diplomacy, especially the most fruitful combinations of

public discussion on the one hand and private negotiations and mediation on the other. I added that the
opportunities are there to be tested and used.

This is a fascinating field where the experience of
classical diplomacy, the successes and the errors of the
League of Nations and of the United Nations, and the
knowledge of the technique and psychology of a public
debate utilizing to the full the modern media, all have to
be taken into account by the political scientist as well as
by those who are put in positions where they have to explore possibilities by action. Looking at my present job
from the point of view of the social scientist, but looking
at it also just as much from the point of view of somebody deeply engaged in the common effort to save peace
and to build a world of peace, I cannot find any part of
my present task more challenging than the one which
consists in trying to develop all the potentialities of that
unique diplomatic instrument which the Charter has
created in the institution called the Secretary-General of
the United Nations.

**A further development of quiet diplomacy
is warranted and would in no way reduce
the value of conference diplomacy**

From address to University of California, 25 June 1955:

The very rules of the game, and the specific position of
the Secretariat inside the system, force the Secretariat in
its activities as representative of the Organization as a
whole to apply what is now often called quiet diplomacy.
Such an activity, in fact, comes very close to that of a
Foreign Office, working along classical lines as a ser-

vant of the Government and of the people – with a discretion and integrity rendered necessary by the fact that none of the interests it is there to safeguard and none of the confidences that it may be privileged to enjoy, is its own property but something entrusted to it by its master, the people.

In the General Assembly, as well as in the Councils, open debate is the rule. The public and the press are admitted to practically all meetings and are able to follow the development of arguments, the evolution of conflicts and the arrival at solutions. The debates cover a ground which in earlier times was mostly reserved for negotiation behind closed doors. They have introduced a new instrument of negotiation, that of conference diplomacy. This instrument has many advantages. It can serve to form public opinion. It can subject national policies and proposals to the sharp tests of world-wide appraisal, thus revealing the strength, or weakness, of a cause that might otherwise have remained hidden. It can activate the sound instincts of the common man in favour of righteous causes. It can educate and guide. But it has, also, weaknesses. There is the temptation to play to the gallery at the expense of solid construction. And there is the risk that positions once taken publicly become frozen, making compromise more difficult.

Thus we find introduced in conference diplomacy an aspect of propaganda and an element of rigidity which may be harmful to sound negotiation. In these circumstances it is natural, and it has been increasingly felt, that the balance to be struck within the United Nations between conference diplomacy and quiet diplomacy – whether directly between representatives of Member governments or in contacts between the Secretary-General and Member governments – has to be carefully measured and maintained. This balance should obviously be established in such a way as to render the Organization as valuable an instrument as possible for the achievement of progress towards peace. It is my feeling that there now is a broader recognition than before of the value of quiet diplomacy within the framework of the Organization as a complement to the conference diplomacy of the public debates. My belief is that a further development in that direction is warranted and would in no way reduce the value of conference diplomacy.

It is in the interest of the Member States that we move further in the application of quiet diplomacy

From address to Members of Parliament, London, 2 April 1958:

Criticism has been directed against the great emphasis which I have in recent years put upon the adaptation of private diplomacy to the multilateral framework of the World Organization in pursuit of the goals of the Charter. But, whether you call it private diplomacy, or quiet diplomacy or something else, I believe it is in the interests of the Member States that we move in this direction.

I would not for a moment suggest that the functions of debate and vote do not have their essential place in world affairs today. Nor would I suggest that any step be taken that would retard the development of an increasingly influential role for a well-informed public opinion in the making of foreign policy. But the United Nations is subject to the same principles as apply to diplomacy in all its forms. Long experience has shown that negotiation in public alone does not produce results. If the United Nations is to serve as an increasingly effective instrument of negotiation, the principles and methods of traditional diplomacy need to be applied more fully alongside its public procedures.

Private diplomacy in the task of peace-making should be more used by the Security Council – with or without the Secretary-General

To turn to a more regular field of United Nations activities, I believe that a greater use of private diplomacy in the work of the Security Council might also yield fruitful results. There is an unused paragraph in the United Nations Charter, Article 28, paragraph 2, which reads: 'The Security Council shall hold periodic meetings at which each of its members may, if it so desires, be represented by a member of the government or by some other specially designated representative.' In his commentary to Parliament at the time the Charter was being considered the then Secretary of State for Foreign Affairs of the United Kingdom said of this paragraph, 'It is by these meetings in particular that governments would be able to carry out the fourth Purpose of the Organization'. This fourth purpose is 'to be a center for harmonizing the actions of nations in the attainment of these common ends'.

I do not suggest any move at this time to give formal effect to this paragraph, but I do think that its application from time to time to the negotiation of appropriate
questions might contribute not only to the processes of

conciliation but also toward developing in a new direction the important role that the Security Council is intended by the Charter to play in the task of peace-making.

[---]

It so happens that the Office of the Secretary-General has a place in many of the examples I have cited. But this need not be so. There are many opportunities open to the Member governments and to their representative organs in the United Nations which do not involve my office for the greater use of private diplomacy of a traditional kind, side-by-side with the public procedures of parliamentary diplomacy, either through the use of additional formal procedures or on a purely informal basis...

Behind closed doors the human factor carries more weight and confidential exchanges are possible even across otherwise impossible frontiers

From address to Students Association, Copenhagen, 2 May 1959:

Over the years, the diplomatic representatives accredited to the United Nations have developed a cooperation and built mutual contacts in dealing with problems they have in common, which in reality make them members of a kind of continuous diplomatic conference, in which they are informally following and able to discuss, on a personal basis, all political questions which are important for the work of the Organization. These continuous informal deliberations do not lend themselves to publicity, and they receive none. But it would be a grave mistake to conclude from this that they are unimportant. On the contrary, the flexible and confidential forms in which these discussions can be pursued have given them a particular value as a complement to other diplomatic contacts and to all the various conferences and public exchanges about which we are being informed through the press and which constitute the normal operating procedures in a more traditional diplomacy.

Public debate in the United Nations is dominated by the same differences among the parties as international political life as a whole. But behind closed doors these differences are diluted. The human factor carries more weight there, and confidential exchanges are possible even across frontiers which otherwise appear impassable.

Non-publicized diplomacy within the United Nations offers a mediating influence by all those interested in peace while free from prestige or national interest

From statement to the press, 19 May 1960:

However, the Organization provides also the framework for continued non-publicized negotiations in which it is possible to play on the whole range of approaches which have grown out of the experience of traditional diplomacy. There is in such non-publicized diplomacy within the UN an additional element of value: the mediating influence of the participation of all those who are vitally interested in peace, while free from an immediate involvement in the issues at stake in terms of prestige or national interest.

**Active preventive diplomacy can be
conducted by the United Nations in situations
where no government or regional organization
would be able to act in the same way**

*Hammarskjöld used the term »active preventive diplomacy« to
describe the good offices of the mission exercised by the Secretary-
General's personal representative in the frontier conflict between
Cambodia and Thailand (see page 96). Once the conflict was solved, Hammarskjöld told a press conference in February 1959:*

You can see how much more efficient and smooth-
working such a technique is than the regular one, which
involves all the meetings and debates, and so on. That is
a good case in point to demonstrate how, pragmatically,
we can find better ways to do the job, without at all de-
parting from the Charter but, so to speak, adjusting the
procedures so as to meet a concrete situation as con-
veniently and efficiently as possible.

*»This effort was something of an innovation«, Hammarskjöld told
the goverment of Thailand, »which has enhanced our possibilities
to assist in other cases and [...] has broken new ground for fruitful
UN assistance to member countries.« (Urquhart, p. 310)*

This action, which may lead to the development of a
new pattern – other governments have made two or
three proposals of a similar nature–is an example of
what I should like to call active preventive diplomacy,
which may be conducted by the United Nations,
through the Secretary-General or in other forms, in
many situations where no government or group of governments and no regional organization would be able to
act in the same way. That such interventions are possi- 137

ble for the United Nations is explained by the fact that in the manner I have indicated, the Organization has begun to gain a certain independent position, and that this tendency has led to the acceptance of an independent political and diplomatic activity on the part of the Secretary-General as the 'neutral' representative of the Organization.

The world and the nation

Everybody today with part of his being belongs to one country – with another part he is a world citizen

From address at Stanford University, 19 June 1955:

Nationalism – internationalism. These abstract words, so often abused, so often misunderstood, cover high ideals and strong emotions, reflect modes of thought and action which shape our world.

We often see the word 'nationalism' used in a derogatory sense. The same is true of the word 'internationalism'. When nationalism connotes, for example, a 'go-it-alone' isolationism, and internationalism an outlook which belittles the significance of national life and of nations as centers of political action and spiritual tradition, the words become contradictory and the attitudes they describe irreconcilable. From such interpretations of the words comes the tendency to think of nationalism as in fundamental conflict with an internationalist attitude.

But other interpretations lead to a quite different result. Nationalism and internationalism, when understood as meaning recognition of the value and the rights of the nation, and of the dependence of the nation on the world, represent essential parts of the mental and spiritual equipment of all responsible men in our time. Everybody today, with part of his being, belongs to one country, with its specific traditions and problems, while with another part he has become a citizen of a world which no longer permits national isolation. Seen in this light there could not be any conflict between nationalism and internationalism, between the nation and the world.

We witness a world revolution from which peoples emerge as new dynamic national states in friendly competition

The question is not either the nation *or* the world. It is, rather, how to serve the world by service to our nation, and how to serve the nation by service to the world.

The dilemma is as old as mankind. There has always been the problem of how to harmonize loyalty to the smaller group, inside which we are working, with loyalty to the larger unit to which this group belongs. However, in our time this problem has taken on new proportions and a new significance. It has also developed aspects unknown to previous generations.

For vast multitudes this is an era when, for the first time, they have fully sensed the rights and responsibilities of free peoples and sovereign nations. It is also the era when freedom and sovereignty for the first time have been actually within their reach. Parallel with great social and economic revolutions within many countries, we witness now a world revolution from which peoples, long dependent on others, begin to emerge as strong, dynamic national states.

We should meet this new enthusiasm with understanding, in full appreciation of the rich gifts it may 140 bring to a world of many nations and peoples in friendly competition. In world affairs such an attitude, which is in line with the great traditions of this country, may be regarded as an expression of true democracy in international life.

We can protect our own national character not by resistance to change and isolation but by self-confident development in free contact with the world

It is a sign of true statesmanship, both in the new countries and in older nations, so to direct national policies as to avoid collisions developing out of unwise reactions to the new forces. History places a burden on our shoulders. The creative urges of the emergent nations are tinged with strong emotions from the past. It is for all of us, denying neither the good nor the ills of that past, to look ahead and not to permit old conflicts to envenom the spirit of the creative work before us.

It is natural that this new situation should provoke a resistance, inspired by the fear that our own country and our own private world might find itself submerged in some global development. And so we find people trying to find ways to isolate themselves from general trends and to build up closed, protected units. We can understand or even sympathize with such a reaction, but we must recognize that if it represents a resistance to change, it is doomed to failure. Such self-sought isolation may persevere for some time. It will not endure forever, and the longer the change is resisted and adjustment shirked, the more violent will be the final reaction when the walls collapse.

The reply to nationalists who wish to remain aloof in

such vain efforts at self-protection is that the way to safeguard what they rightly want to defend is not isolation. The way is a vigorous and self-confident development, in free contact with the world, of the special qualities and assets of their nation and their people – a development which should give them their just weight in the international balance. Giving thus to the world what is specifically ours, we could manifest and protect our national character, while accepting change and opening our minds to the influences of the world.

The United Nations is an expression of our will to find a synthesis between the nation and the world

The United Nations is an expression of our will to find a synthesis between the nation and the world, overcoming the one-sidedness reflected in the words of Schiller and Carlyle. It is an attempt to provide us with a framework inside which it is possible to serve the world by serving our nation, and to serve our nation by serving the world. Whatever may be the past shortcomings of this experiment in world organization, it gives sense and direction to the efforts of all men who are striving towards a better world. The Organization was born out of the cataclysms of the second World War. It should justify the sacrifices of all fighters for freedom and justice in that war. I remember the bitter lines of a great Anglo-American poet who writes in an 'Epitaph on an Unknown Soldier':

To save your world, you asked this man to die,
Would this man, could he see you now, ask why?*

It is our duty to the past, and it is our duty to the future, so to serve both our nations and the world as to be able to give a reply to that anguished question.

*W. H. Auden

Now the national interest merges naturally into the international interest

From address to Members of Parliament, London, 2 April 1958:

Now the lines between national and international policy have begun to blur. What is in the national interest, when truly seen, merges naturally into the international interest.

I am reminded of a memorandum written in 1907 by Mr. Eyre Crowe for the British Foreign Office. He advised then that Britain's best safeguard for the future would be a national policy that is 'so directed as to harmonize with the general desires and ideals common to all mankind, and more particularly that... is closely identified with the primary and vital interests of a majority, or as many as possible, of the other nations'.

This seems to me to be a policy – and a principle – which it would be both right and wise for all nations to seek to follow. It is, in effect, the policy and the principle of the United Nations Charter.

The world is a spiritual thing

**We cannot mould the world as masters of
a material thing but we can influence the development
of the world from within as a spiritual thing**

*From address to American Association for the United Nations, 14
September 1953:*

In the classical Chinese collection of poetic philosophy,
ascribed to Tao Tse-Tung, it is said somewhere that
whoever wants to grip the world and shape it will fail,
because the world is a spiritual thing that cannot be
shaped. On first reaction, this might seem to be the an-
tithesis of the spirit that animated Columbus. But this is
not so. The history of mankind is made by man, but
men partly make it blindly. No one can foresee with cer-
tainty what will emerge from the give and take of the
forces at work in any age. For that reason history often
seems to run its course beyond the reach of any man or
nation. We cannot mould the world as masters of a
material thing. Columbus did not reach the East Indies.
But we can influence the development of the world from
within as a spiritual thing. In this sense Columbus
would have been a pioneer for a new age even if he himself had never reached America.

As individuals and as groups we can put our influence
to the best of our understanding and ability on the side
of what we believe is right and true. We can help in the
movement toward those ends that inspire our lives and

are shared by all men of good will – in terms very close to those of the Charter of the United Nations – peace and freedom for all, in a world of equal rights for all.

Church – State

**The future may be one of a struggle between
the State trying to make itself Church
and the Church trying to make itself State**

*From address to American Associaton for the United Nations,
New York, 14 September 1953:*

When I think of the work before us – you as friends and
believers in the United Nations, and I as Secretary-General
– I am reminded of a famous idea of Dostoevsky
in *The Brothers Karamazov,* where he has one of his
heroes say that the future may be one of a struggle between
the State trying to make itself Church and the
Church trying to make itself State.

Applied in international life today, we might say that
the United Nations represents ideals at least professed
by all nations, but that it is not a super-state trying to
impose on people any 'right' way of life or any way of
life different from one freely chosen by the people. On
the contrary, it seeks as the repository and voice of a
common heritage of ideals to penetrate the life of states
in their international relations and to influence their
conduct toward a wider realization of those ideals.

**The Secretariat and the Secretary-General
are representatives of a secular church of ideas
and principles in international affairs**

Thus you see that I conceive the Secretariat and the Secretary-General in their relations with the governments
as representatives of a secular 'church' of ideals and
principles in international affairs of which the United
Nations is the expression.

In a different way those who belong to organized citizens' groups supporting the United Nations in all countries, represent this secular 'church' to their respective
national states. It is your role to influence opinion within the circle to which your reach extends toward the
course you believe to be right for your country. Whether
your circle be small or large, it counts, for it is the sum
total of all of them that influences the policies of governments.

Your role is different from mine in this respect.
Whereas the international civil servant speaks for the
ideals and commitments of the Charter as they may affect the formulation of national policies, you speak for
the national interest of your countries in their policies
toward and in the United Nations. This is important.
You are rightly partisans for the best interests of your
country as you see them. When you speak and act for
national policies that will strengthen the influence of the
United Nations you are doing so because you believe
that this is best for your country as well as for humanity.

Your role is of the highest significance. No matter
what their private judgment, those in positions of authority cannot go against prevailing public opinion or

lead in a direction the public is not prepared to follow. Your influence in what you believe to be the right direction, exercised in the manifold ways that are available to you, is essential to the exercise of statesmanship.

I know there are many occasions when the pressures and the events that lead in the contrary direction seem overwhelming. But just as we cannot shape our world at will like a handful of clay, neither do such pressures and events inexorably lead on to a preordained doom. They are subject to influence and change.

Human rights

The final issue is what dignity
we are willing to give to man

From address at Johns Hopkins University, 14 June 1955:

In the fight for freedom which puts its stamp so strongly on present-day life, the final issue is what dignity we are willing to give to man. It is part of the American creed, part of the inherited ideology of all Western civilization, that each man is an end in himself, of infinite value as an individual. To pay lip-service to this view or to invoke it in favour of our actions is easy. But what is in fact the central tenet of this ideology becomes a reality only when we, ourselves, follow a way of life, individually and as members of a group, which entitles us personally to the freedom of a mature individual, living under the rules of his conscience. And it becomes the key to our dealings with others only when inspired by a faith which in truth and spirit gives to them the value which is theirs according to what we profess to be our creed.

The Universal Declaration of Human Rights is an
international synthesis of the thinking of our generation

From address at Williamsburg, Va., 14 May 1956:

The Charter of the United Nations calls for international cooperation in 'promoting and encouraging respect for human rights and for fundamental freedoms for all

without distinction as to race, sex, language or religion.'
At the San Francisco Conference eleven years ago, a determined effort was made to incorporate a Bill of Rights in the Charter. However, it was realized that the task was beyond the capacity of a relatively short conference. It was therefore decided that it would not be done until the international organization had been established.

Three years later the Universal Declaration of Human Rights was a fact. This Declaration enunciates not only all the traditional political rights and civil liberties, but also economic, social and cultural rights. It is an international synthesis of the thinking of our generation on these questions. Unlike the Virginia Declaration, which was drawn up by George Mason, there is no one person who can be identified as the principal draftsman of the Universal Declaration. The Declaration is anonymous in its character, and back of it we find literally thousands of people who directly and indirectly participated actively in its drafting. Also for that reason it may be called the universal expression in the field of human rights of the aims of our world of today, a world where the memory is still fresh of some of the worst infringements of human rights ever experienced in history, and a world which is also facing the problem of human rights in new and increasingly complicated forms.

The goal for the individual as well as for governments must be the recognition in action of the dignity of man and of the sanctity of those freedoms which follow from such recognition

The Universal Declaration is not, of course, a treaty and has, in itself, no force in law. But, as 'a common standard of achievement for all peoples and all nations,' it not only crystallizes the political thought of our times on these matters, but it has also influenced the thinking of legislators all over the world. It is in this sense a worthy successor to the long line of affirmations of human liberties which began here in Williamsburg, though it is not and cannot be the final word in these questions, which by their very nature are as dynamic as life itself.

The relationship of man to society is a relationship for which every generation must seek to find the proper form. But, just as ideas far back in the past gave direction to the efforts for the best in former times, so this declaration should give direction to those who now carry the responsibility for a sound development of society.

As it stands, the Universal Declaration of Human Rights is both a symbol of the magnitude of the problem of human rights in our century and a measure of the concern with the problem which is shared by the governments and peoples represented in the United Nations. But it is also, in words for our time, a reminder of what must be the goal for the individual as well as for governments; the recognition in action of the dignity of man and of the sanctity of those freedoms which follow from such recognition.

Without recognition of human rights
we shall never have peace

From address to American Jewish Committee, New York 10 April 1957:

Arthur Waley quotes what an early Chinese historian had to say about the philosopher Sung Tzu and his followers, some 350 years B.C. To one who works in the United Nations, the quotation strikes a familiar note. It runs as follows:

'Constantly rebuffed but never discouraged, they went round from State to State helping people to settle their differences, arguing against wanton attack and pleading for the suppression of arms, that the age in which they lived might be saved from its state of continual war. To this end they interviewed princes and lectured the common people, nowhere meeting with any great success, but obstinately persisting in their task, till kings and commoners alike grew weary of listening to them. Yet undeterred they continued to force themselves on people's attention.' /.../

We can learn from his attitude, both in our efforts to move towards peace and in our work for universal recognition of human rights.

We know that the question of peace and the question of human rights are closely related. Without recognition of human rights we shall never have peace, and it is only within the framework of peace that human rights can be fully developed.

An obligation for the United Nations to assist governments in safeguarding the most elementary of human rights: the right of everyone to security and freedom from fear

In fact, the work for peace is basically a work for the most elementary of human rights: the right of everyone to security and to freedom from fear. We, therefore, recognize it as one of the first duties of a government to take measures in order to safeguard for its citizens this very right. But we also recognize it as an obligation for the emerging world community to assist governments in safeguarding this elementary human right without having to lock themselves in behind the wall of arms.

The dilemma of our age, with its infinite possibilities of self-destruction, is how to grow out of the world of armaments into a world of international security, based on law. We are only at the very beginning of such a change. The natural distrust in the possibility of progress is nourished by unavoidable set-backs and, when distrust is thus strengthened, this in turn increases our difficulties.

The effort may seem hopeless. It will prove hopeless unless we, all of us, show the persistence of Sung Tzu and his followers, and unless peoples and governments alike are willing to take smaller immediate risks in order to have a better chance to avoid the final disaster threatening us if we do not manage to turn the course of developments in a new direction. [...]

In its present phase the Organization may look to many like a preacher who cannot impose the law he states or realize the gospel he interprets. [...] It is easy to say that it is pointless to state the law if it cannot be enforced. However, to do so is to forget that if the law is the inescapable law of the future, it would be treason to the future not to state the law simply because of the difficulties of the present. Indeed, how could it ever become a living reality if those who are responsible for its development were to succumb to the immediate difficulties arising when it is still a revolutionary element in the life of society?

Solidarity

**The democratic ideals which demand
equal opportunities for all should be applied
also to peoples and races**

From address at University of Lund, 4 May 1959:

The health and strength of a community depend on every citizen's feeling of solidarity with the other citizens, and on his willingness, in the name of this solidarity, to shoulder his part of the burdens and responsibilities of the community. The same is of course true of humanity as a whole. And just as it cannot be argued that within a community an economic upper class holds its favoured position by virtue of greater ability, as a quality which is, as it were, vested in the group by nature, so it is, of course, impossible to maintain this in regard to nations in their mutual relationships.

I believe that no anthropologist nowadays would say that the various branches of the family of man represent fundamentally different potentialities for contributions and development in various fields of intellectual and material activity. If I may speak on the basis of my own experience, which in one way is of course limited, but in another very extensive, I would say that for my part I have not been able to discover any such differences.

We thus live in a world where, no more internationally than nationally, can any distinct group claim superiority in mental gifts and potentialities of development. What 157 may in practice seem to point in another direction is explained by the vast differences which have prevailed in opportunity to bring the gifts to fruition and expression. Those democratic ideals which demand equal opportunities for all should be applied also to peoples and races.

In these circumstances, it appears evident that no nation or group of nations can base its future on a claim of supremacy. It is in its own interest that the other groups have opportunities equal to those it has had itself. To contribute to this is an act of solidarity which is not only good for the whole but, in the long run, rebounds to the advantage even of those who take the action.

**A world of order and justice will never be ours
without foundation in international law**

From address at University of California, 25 June 1955:

Between sovereign nations conflicts arise to a large
extent in a political context. But the substance of the
disputes is also often in fact a question of law. While it is
natural that the conflicts tend to be treated in forms adequate to political problems, it is also true that they could
be resolved on a basis of law much more frequently than
is now the case. If the position of the judiciary inside the
international constitutional system so far is weak, in
practice, this may be explained primarily by the fact
that it often seems most safe for a sovereign state to
tackle a problem as a matter for political reconciliation.
The system of international law is still fairly undeveloped and there are wide margins of uncertainty. Why,
one may ask, run the risk of a possibly less favourable
outcome reached on the basis of law instead of a more
advantageous one that might be achieved by skillful negotiation and under the pressure of political arguments.
Why? Is not the reason obvious? First of all, is it not in
the interest of sound development to restrict as much as
possible the arena where strength is an argument and to
put as much as possible under the rule of law? But there
is a further consideration. If we regret the undeveloped
state of international law, should we not use all possibil- 159

ities to develop an international common law by submitting our conflicts to jurisdiction wherever that is possible? I apologize for having gone into these matters, so ably and with such competence covered here by Judge Hackworth. I have done so only because it appears to me on the basis of daily experience that the world of order and justice for which we are striving will never be ours unless we are willing to give it the broadest possible and the firmest possible foundation in law.

Institutional systems of international coexistence are in an embryonic stage

From address at University of Chicago, 1 May 1960:

International law, in spite of the vast literature covering the subject, has on the whole been less favoured by serious students than national law. And within the field of international law what might be called international constitutional law and its specific problems has attracted less interest than other parts with their far longer history in the Western world. In fact, international constitutional law is still in an embryonic stage; we are still in the transition between institutional systems of international coexistence and constitutional systems of international cooperation. It is natural that, at such a stage of transition, theory is still vague, mixed with elements of a political nature and dependent on what basically may be considered sociological theory.

Men organize themselves into families. The families join together in villages or tribes. The tribes and the villages fuse into peoples, and one day, out of the self-consciousness of a people, there develops a feeling of difference and separateness, the positive expression of which is a feeling of nationhood. The nation organizes its life within a set of constitutional rules, evolving in practice or crystallized as law. Under the constitution the people develop national organs with different functions and a division of responsibilities representing a balance of power. Through those organs laws are given, setting the pattern for the lives and activities of the individuals and the groups which constitute the nation.

Is that the end of the road of the development of human society? Of course not. Nation borders on nation, peoples get in touch with each other, and whatever differences there may exist and whatever conflicts of interest the people may see, they are forced to live together, fighting or in peace, as neighbours with limits put by nature to their possible self-sufficiency and for that reason with a need to develop forms for international intercourse, permitting more or less highly developed degrees of cooperation. So an institutional system of coexistence is developed with its rules and practices. Still there is no international society. Still the nation remains the highest fully organized form for the life of peoples.

The perspective of biological evolution gives us a broader and more organic sense of the role of law

However primitive a basic institutional pattern may be, it carries within it seeds for the growth of higher social organisms, covering wider areas and groups of peoples. To use my terminology of a moment ago, such an institutional system for coexistence, stage by stage, may be developed and enriched until, on single points or on a broad front, it passes over into a constitutional system of cooperation. When that happens, we get in a first, necessarily rudimentary form, a form of society which, while preserving and protecting the lives of the nations, points towards an international constitutional system surmounting the nations, utilizing them to the extent that smaller units are more efficient instruments for evolution, but creating rules which limit the influence of the nations in fields where bigger units present greater possibilities for development and survival.

I believe it is useful, in the discussion of the development of human society, be it national or international, to keep in mind this sociological perspective taken over from theories of biological evolution. It is a perspective which helps us to a more realistic appraisal of what it is we have achieved and what it is we are trying to do, as well as of the scope and significance of our failures and our successes. It also gives us a broader and more organic sense of the role of law – again I use the word in its broadest sense, including not only written law but the whole social pattern of established rules of action and behaviour – making us see the differences as well as the similarities between the national and international field, and warning us against false analogies.

World government

**World organization is necessary to national life
but we are far from ripe for world government**

From address at Stanford University, 19 June 1955:

We undoubtedly need world organization, but we are
far from ripe for world government. Indeed, even modest attempts at regional 'integration' have met with considerable difficulties, not because of any superstitious
respect for national sovereignty, but because the peoples
want to know in whose hands they put their fate, if they
are to surrender part of their self-determination as
nations. Further: how often have we not seen those who
most eagerly plead for integration among other countries themselves shrink back from even the slightest
discipline of their own sovereign rights?

Discussion about international integration, world
organization and world government throws much light
on the problem of the nation versus the world. I would
not regard the widespread and often vocal resistance to
anything which might be construed as tending to limit
national sovereignty as a new upsurge of nationalism. It
should rather be regarded as a symptom of how heavily
faith in national self-determination weighs in the scales
in every effort to reconcile the nation and the world.
Such expression of national feelings is both an asset and
a liability. It is an asset to the extent that it reflects the
determination to shape one's own fate and to take the

responsibility for it. It is an asset as a brake on immature experiments in international integration. But it is a liability when it blinds our eyes to the necessity of that degree of international organization which has become necessary to national life.

Step by step we pave the way for the society of the future – not by the construction of ideal patterns to be imposed on society

From address at University of Chicago, 1 May 1960:

Those who advocate world government, and this or that special form of world federalism, often present challenging theories and ideas, but we, like our ancestors, can only press against the receding wall which hides the future. It is by such efforts, pursued to the best of our ability, more than by the construction of ideal patterns to be imposed upon society, that we lay the basis and pave the way for the society of the future.

Regional integration

The institutional evolution in European cooperation makes it imperative to push forward institutionally and, eventually, constitutionally, without preconceived ideas of the ultimate form

From address at University of Chicago, 1 May 1960:

In a galaxy of nations like the European one, there are, of course, strongly ingrained patterns and inherited sets of rules which integrate the area. The life of those nations develops within a system explained by a number of shared interests and basic concepts, which set a framework for trade, for travel and exchange of people, for movement of capital and for exchange of ideas. Within the system created by those rules we have, in a sense, a kind of 'common market', which, however, does not infringe on the sovereignty of any of the nations forming part of the market and which, therefore, still lacks completely what might be called a constitutional element. It thus remains a purely institutional pattern. With the recent creation of the European Common Market of six nations, the Coal and Steel Community, and similar bodies, a decisive step has been taken in the further development of this institutional framework. In fact, by these actions the system has been pushed beyond the border of institutional arrangements and has come to include some initial constitutional elements.

The institutional evolution in Europe has brought us a step in the direction of a true constitutional framework for cooperation which, through experimental stages of a confederal nature, may finally lead to some kind of federal system or even stronger forms of association. However, just as in the case of world federalism, I think it is wise to avoid talking of this or that kind of ultimate political target and to realize that the development is still in an early stage of institutional evolution, although a few vanguard penetrations into the constitutional area have taken place. What seems imperative is to push forward institutionally and, eventually, constitutionally all along the line, guided by current needs and experiences, without preconceived ideas of the ultimate form.

The United Nations represents an elaboration of an institutional pattern of coexistence with points reaching into the constitutional sphere

It is known that Sir Winston Churchill, in his time, advocated an approach to the building of a world community through the creation of regional organizations as stepping-stones to more highly developed forms of international coexistence or cooperation. We see instead the advance being made in part only through regional arrangements, but in part – and mainly – independently of such arrangements and directly on the basis of universality. If Sir Winston's line had been followed, it would, with my terminology, have meant that regional organizations step by step would have developed a basic
institutional pattern for universal coexistence by which,

later on, a push forward, on the universal level, could have been tried in the direction of a constitutional pattern.

If we accept the interpretation given here to the European community and the French-African community, the United Nations could, in a similar sense, be called a 'community', although of a universal character. It represents in itself, with the methods of operation and the rules established, an elaboration of an institutional pattern of coexistence. It even has, in theory, points where it reaches into the constitutional sphere; I have, of course, in mind especially the authority given to the Security Council to act with mandatory power, provided the action is supported unanimously by the permanent members. However, as is natural with a more complex system, built up of a greater number of components, among which – to use the language of natural science – in many fields forces of repulsion tend to balance or outbalance forces of attraction, the cohesion is more unstable and the field covered by the institutional pattern less extended or more marginal than in the case of regional groupings.

Unless steps are taken to increase the effectiveness of action within the United Nations, the danger will exist that the strengthening of regional economic organizations may divide as much as it unites

From statement to Economic and Social Council, 6 June, 1960:

Regional arrangements among neighbouring or like-minded countries are bound to play a major role in the formulation of international economic policies. Never-   167 theless, it would be far from realistic to assume that regional arrangements can alone suffice to cope with the urgent problems confronting the community of nations. The United Nations organization remains the only universal agency in which countries with widely differing political institutions and at different stages of economic development may exchange views, share their problems and experiences, probe each other's reactions to policies of mutual interest, and initiate collective action; it is inspired and bound by the solemn pledge of the Charter to take 'joint' as well as 'separate' action. Unless steps are now taken to increase the effectiveness of action within the United Nations, the danger will exist that the strengthening of regional economic organs outside the Organization may divide as much as it unites.

If regional arrangements fall within the sphere of bloc conflicts, they may lead to a weakening of the uniting force of the common interest and aggravate the split

From Introduction to the Annual Report 1959–1960:

For the first time in history, the concept of a world economy has come to take on a significant meaning not only for the student of economics but also for the statesman and the layman.

Unfortunately, this growing interdependence has recently been reflected much less in efforts and activities within the United Nations than outside it. The United Nations can welcome regional arrangements among neighbouring or like-minded countries. As long as such arrangements are so designed as to reinforce rather than

to supplant the common effort towards establishing

conditions of economic and social progress, they have an important role to play. A real danger arises, however, when such regional arrangements are so envisaged as to make them fall within the sphere of bloc conflict. In that case, efforts which properly should embody and be supported by a common interest may instead lead to a weakening of the uniting force of that interest and aggravate the split. This, obviously, is the reverse of the major purpose and function of the United Nations in its efforts to provide for a growing measure of political stability.

Community of power

**As an idealist Woodrow Wilson wished to end
the old system of the balance of power
and substitute it with a community of power**

*In an address at New York University, 20 May 1956, Hammar-
skjöld discussed idealism and realism when judging the world
organization:*

In our day too, we often hear it said that the United Nations has succeeded here, or has failed there. What do
we mean ? Do we refer to the purposes of the Charter?
They are expressions of universally shared ideals which
cannot fail us, though we, alas, often fail them. Or do
we think of the institutions of the United Nations? They
are our tools. We fashioned them. We use them. It is our
responsibility to remedy any flaws there may be in them.
It is our responsibility to correct any failures in our use
of them. And we must expect the responsibility for reme-
dying the flaws and correcting the failures to go on and
on, as long as human beings are imperfect and human
institutions likewise.

This is a difficult lesson for both idealists and realists,
though for different reasons. I suppose that, just as the
first temptation of the realist is the illusion of cynicism,
so the first temptation of the idealist is the illusion of
Utopia. As an idealist, it was natural that Woodrow
Wilson also did not entirely escape this temptation, any
more than have most of the idealists of history. In his

valiant fight for the cause of the League of Nations, he went beyond the concept of an institution acting for the common interest of the peoples of the world. He visualized the establishment of the League as ending the old system of the balance of power and substituting what he called a 'community of power'.

True collective security to defend world peace is to be found at the end, not the beginning, of the effort to create world institutions

The creation of a true community of power to serve the common interest is, indeed, the goal – now as it was in Woodrow Wilson's day. But the establishment of the League of Nations did not, and could not, of itself bring such a community of power into being. It did not, nor could it, end at one stroke the system of the balance of power in international affairs.

The League was an association of sovereign nation-states, just as the United Nations is today. In such an association, the play of the balance of power is inevitable. And it should be said that one of the most serious remaining obstacles in the way of public understanding of the true role of the United Nations today results from a similar tendency to picture the United Nations of 1945 as establishing collective security for the world.

Now, as then, it is important for all of us to understand that true collective security, in the sense of an international police power engaged to defend the peace of the world, is to be found at the end, not at the beginning, of the effort to create and use world institutions 172 that are effective in the service of the common interest.

The spirit and practice of world community must first gain in strength and custom by processes of organic growth. It is to the helping along of these processes of growth that we should devote all our ingenuity and our effort. To the extent that we are able to increase the weight of the common interest as against the weight of special interests, and therefore of the power of the whole community to guide the course of events, we shall be approaching that much nearer to the goal.

The United Nations and the Cold War

**To keep problems outside the Cold War orbit
and to lift problems out of this orbit is a
natural function for the Secretary-General**

*What role might the United Nations play in developing a thaw in
the Cold War? This question was often put to the Secretary-General who answered in different contexts. From statement at press
conference, 5 February 1959:*

I do believe that the United Nations in fact is serving the
purpose of thawing the Cold War the whole time, and I
do believe that to the extent that such a thaw may come
about, the United Nations will increasingly be a focal
point for that development.

It is quite natural, as you know, in this very room and
in the lobbies here, there are, after all, contacts which in
themselves are a denial of the state of absolute frozen-
ness, because they do represent human contacts, they do
represent, at the least, an attempt at a meeting of minds,
and they are, I think, very often imbued by and inspired
by a spirit of personal confidence, even if the general
temperature may be very low in the sense that it is characterized by, so to say, official lack of confidence /.../

I might perhaps express it this way: that I consider it a
very natural function for the Secretary-General to keep
problems as much as possible outside the Cold War
orbit and on the other hand, of course, to lift problems
out of the Cold War orbit to all the extent he can. That

is for many reasons. One of them is that it is one way in which we can get over the difficulties created for the United Nations and United Nations operations by the Cold War. It is one way, so to say, if not to thaw the Cold War, at least to limit its impact on international life.

International conflicts in areas not committed in the major conflict may be solved in agreement with the big powers

From Introduction to the Annual Report 1959–1960:

One word may, however, be said about the possibilities of substantive action by the United Nations in a split world.

Fundamental though the differences splitting our world are, the areas which are not committed in the major conflicts are still considerable. Whether the countries concerned call themselves non-committed, neutral, neutralist or something else, they have all found it not to be in harmony with their role and interests in world politics to tie their policies, in a general sense, to any one of the blocs or to any specific line of action supported by one of the sides in the major conflict. The reasons for such attitudes vary. That, however, is less important in this special context than the fact that conflicts arising within the non-committed areas offer opportunities for solutions which avoid an aggravation of big Power differences and can remain uninfluenced by them. There is thus a field within which international conflicts may be faced and solved with such harmony between the power blocs as was anticipated as a condition for Security

Council action in San Francisco. Agreement may be

achieved because of a mutual interest among the big Powers to avoid having a regional or local conflict drawn into the sphere of bloc politics.

In the case of conflicts on the margin of or inside the sphere of bloc differences, the United Nations should seek to bring such conflicts out of this sphere through solutions aiming at their localization in order to avoid an extension or to achieve a reduction of the bloc conflict area

With its constitution and structure, it is extremely difficult for the United Nations to exercise an influence on problems which are clearly and definitely within the orbit of present day conflicts between power blocs. If a specific conflict is within that orbit, it can be assumed that the Security Council is rendered inactive, and it may be feared that even positions taken by the General Assembly would follow lines strongly influenced by considerations only indirectly related to the concrete difficulty under consideration. Whatever the attitude of the General Assembly and the Security Council, it is in such cases also practically impossible for the Secretary-General to operate effectively with the means put at his disposal, short of risking seriously to impair the usefulness of his office for the Organization in all the other cases for which the services of the United Nations Secretariat are needed.

This clearly defines the main field of useful activity of the United Nations in its efforts to prevent conflicts or to solve conflicts. Those efforts must aim at keeping newly arising conflicts outside the sphere of bloc differences. Further, in the case of conflicts on the margin of, or inside, the sphere of bloc differences, the United Nations should seek to bring such conflicts out of this sphere through solutions aiming, in the first instance, at their strict localization. In doing so, the Organization and its agents have to lay down a policy line, but this will then not be for one party against another, but for the general purpose of avoiding an extension or achieving a reduction of the area into which the bloc conflicts penetrate.

In the Congo the United Nations has tried to counter tendencies to introduce the big power conflict into Africa and put the younger African countries under the shadow of the Cold War.

From statement on UN operations in the Congo before the Security Council, 15 February 1961:

Violent and vocal attacks on the Organization have come from both sides. The main accusation was a lack of objectivity. The historian will undoubtedly find in this balance of accusations the very evidence of that objectivity we were accused of lacking, but also of the fact that very many Member nations have not yet accepted the limits put on their national ambitions by the very existence of the United Nations and by the membership of that Organization.

Now, under basically identical although superficially more dramatic circumstances, we have again reached the point where a local armed conflict is threatening in forms which are only too likely to lead to a widening of

the conflict into the international arena. I have no new

solutions to offer to you. Still, I firmly believe that, as in July and August last year, the only way in which the continent of Africa and its countries can counter a tragic development into an international conflict, perhaps on a world-wide scale, is by rallying around common aims within the framework of the United Nations.

African solidarity within the United Nations was the reply to the threats last year; I am firmly convinced that it still is the only reply.

UN presence

The United Nations enters to fill a vacuum so as to prevent action from any of the major parties

»United Nations presence« was coined at the time of Hammar-skjöld as a diplomatic concept to describe preventive UN actions in conflict areas where a power vacuum had been created or ran the risk of being created. From Introduction to the Annual Report 1959–1960:

Experience indicates that the preventive diplomacy, to which the efforts of the United Nations must thus to a large extent be directed, is of special significance in cases where the original conflict may be said either to be the result of, or to imply risks for, the creation of a power vacuum between the main blocs. Preventive action in such cases must in the first place aim at filling the vacuum so that it will not provoke action from any of the major parties, the initiative for which might be taken for preventive purposes but might in turn lead to counter-action from the other side. The ways in which a vacuum can be filled by the United Nations so as to forestall such initiatives differ from case to case, but they have this in common: temporarily, and pending the filling of a vacuum by normal means, the United Nations enters the picture on the basis of its non-commitment to any power bloc, so as to provide to the extent possible a guarantee in relation to all parties against initiatives from others.

The special need and the special possibilities for what I here call preventive United Nations diplomacy have been demonstrated in several recent cases, such as Suez and Gaza, Lebanon and Jordan, Laos and the Congo.

A study of the records of the conflicts to which I have just referred shows how it has been possible to use the means and methods of the United Nations for the purposes I have indicated. In all cases, whatever the immediate reason for the United Nations initiative, the Organization has moved so as to forestall developments which might draw the specific conflict, openly or actively, into the sphere of power bloc differences. It has done so by introducing itself into the picture, sometimes with very modest means, sometimes in strength, so as to eliminate a political, economic and social, or military vacuum.

The United Nations presence in the Congo is justified by the vision of the international community to avoid this important area being split by bloc conflicts

The view expressed here as to the special possibilities and responsibilities of the Organization in situations of a vacuum has reached an unusually clear expression in the case of the Congo. There, the main argument presented for United Nations intervention was the breakdown of law and order, the rejection of the attempt to maintain order by foreign troops, and the introduction of the United Nations Force so as to create the basis for the withdrawal of the foreign troops and for the forestalling of initiatives to introduce any other foreign troops into the territory with the obvious risks for widening international conflict which would ensue.

Whether the Congo operation is characterized as a case of preventive diplomacy, or as a move in order to fill a vacuum and to forestall the international risks created by the development of such a vacuum, or as a policy aimed at the localization of a conflict with potentially wide international repercussions, is not essential. Whatever the description, the political reality remains. It is a policy which is justified by the wish of the international community to avoid this important area being split by bloc conflicts. It is a policy rendered possible by the fact that both blocs have an interest in avoiding such an extension of the area of conflict because of the threatening consequences, were the localization of the conflict to fail.

By preventing the widening of the geographical and political area of the conflict, the United Nations makes a significant contribution in settling the differences between the power blocs

Thus the Organization in fact also exercises a most important, though indirect, influence on the conflicts between the power blocs by preventing the widening of the geographical and political area covered by these conflicts and by providing for solutions whenever the interests of all parties in a localization of conflict can be mobilized in favour of its efforts.

The Organization in this way also makes a significant contribution in the direction of an ultimate solution of the differences between the power blocs, as it is obvious that it is a condition for an improvement in the situation 183 that the area to which those differences apply, as a minimum requirement, is not permitted to expand and, so far as possible, is reduced.

East and West

A natural difference of view

At a Canadian Television press conference, 7 March 1956, a journalist referring to a statement by Hammarskjöld about the very high standing that the United Nations enjoys in Asia, asked him: »You spoke of the man in the street, who sometimes considers the United Nations as a bulwark against tyranny and exploitation. Is there any way that this feeling which you gathered during your trip could be conveyed to the developed nations of the world, where sometimes, as we all know, the United Nations is thought of as a poor relative?« Hammarskjöld answered as follows:

I think we must look at this in the light of historical developments, and I should like to put my answer in a somewhat paradoxical way. It is natural for old and well-established countries to see in the United Nations a limitation on their sovereignty. It is just as natural that a young country, a country emerging on the world stage, should find in the United Nations an addition to its sovereignty, an added means of speaking to the world. That difference between the two approaches is basic and is easily explained, I think, by historical circumstances and present political problems.

You complain indirectly of the somewhat high-handed way in which, perhaps, the United Nations is sometimes treated and discussed in some countries. I would not complain about it, because I think it is perfectly natural – just as I regard the reaction of many countries in the East as being natural. But I think that to whatever extent Asian people and, to some degree, I myself, as a

185

kind of indirect spokesman for Asian people, can make it clearer to the Western countries that the United Nations comes into the picture in this way in a very great part of the world, to that extent we will smooth out this curious difference and at the same time bring about a realistic appraisal of the United Nations in political terms, so that you will reach your result in the long run. But I would not like to preach to the Western countries that you are criticizing. I would just like to bring home to them the natural difference of view which is represented by the Asian countries.

The future will attach greater importance to the rebirth of Asia and Africa in the historical evolution of the present epoch than to the questions now uppermost in the news

After a long journey in Asia in the spring of 1959, Hammarskjöld addressed the Academic Association of the University of Lund, Sweden, 4 May 1959, where he paid attention to the differences in the scales of values in Asia and the West:

In one of the capitals of the Orient – one of the smallest and least accessible ones – I had a conversation recently which happened to turn on questions of religion. This happens often in that part of the world. All about us, there was a row of pagodas from different centuries, and life was strongly colored by the position of the city as a Buddhist shrine. But the representative of the country with whom I was talking said that for many Buddhism was hardly more than a thin cloak over animism. He added: 'But what is there for you as a Scandinavian to say? Think of Knut Hamsun or Selma Lagerlöf!'

The story may serve as a starting point for some thoughts about the confrontation of East and West in present-day international life, and the problems posed by this confrontation. No matter how overwhelming other world problems may appear to us because of their proximity, it is possible that the future will attach greater importance to the rebirth of Asia and Africa in the historical evolution of the present epoch, than to the questions now uppermost in the news.

The little anecdote has many illuminating points, important to an understanding of the situation. It offers an instance of how much an educated Asian may know of Western culture – far more than the Westerner generally knows about that of Asia. At the same time, the reaction is typical of the matter-of-fact way in which references to religion may be made by leaders in a part of the world, where yet, without exception, religion is a dominant political factor. Another aspect worth noting is the one apparent in the semi-ironical equating of spiritual development in East and West. Finally – even though the anecdote shows this only indirectly – conversations like this one offer striking proof of how openly a discussion can be conducted between a Westerner and today's spokesmen of Asia or Africa. We have advanced far beyond the world once mirrored by Kipling or Sven Hedin.

The Asian is not willing to pay for the improvement of living conditions by changing his way of life

A related difficulty is created by the differences in the scales of values. In the eyes of the East – and perhaps in actual reality – the overwhelming technical progress which is the mark of the West has marked us more than we ourselves realize. The Asian admires the material achievements of the West, he knows what they may mean for the improvement of living conditions in his own world, and he is anxious to make use of their results. But he is not willing to pay for the improvement by changing his way of life in a manner which may seem to him an unavoidable concomitant of technical progress, but incompatible with the spirit and traditions of his own people.

Poverty is relative. When life has been made safe and elementary needs filled, people are hardly made happier by being exposed to influences creating needs which fundamentally are foreign to them and tend to grow more rapidly than new means of satisfying the needs can be created. This is no argument for the contentedness of the poor as it was worshipped in the Victorian fairy-tale world. Nor is it a question of the poverty which is borne with equanimity because it is shared by all. What we must remember in this connection is that strong and living spiritual traditions in the Afro-Asian world still make for an approach to life and its blessings which vouchsafes happiness on a level where we would speak of misery. The obligation of all of us, and of the international community, to give economic security and raise the living standards for those two-thirds of humanity who live close to the level of starvation or below it, is inescapable. But the representative, for instance, of the Buddhist world is more conscious than we are of how true it is, even in the most elemental context of everyday life, that man lives not by bread alone.

**The spiritual heritage of the West may be difficult
to enjoy for the Asian without a sense of cleavage
which may be pushed to rootlessness**

Finally, there are difficulties explained by the fact that
we are still very close to the epoch when the West lived
happily in its feeling of superiority, thus innocently creating a corresponding uncertainty in minds and hearts
of representatives of other cultural regions. For an
Asian or an African, it may be difficult to enjoy the spiritual heritage of the West without a sense of cleavage
which may be pushed all the way to rootlessness, or
without an uneasiness as though in the face of treason,
while the Westerner, from his point of view, may widen
his cultural range and absorb other traditions without
corresponding tensions. Here we meet what may be the
most serious of the obstacles to be surmounted. Can we
solve the problem without, as it were, *growing* out of it,
the way we do when the same kind of difficulties occur
in our personal lives? Here, the greater responsibility
rests on him who believes he is the stronger.

**We must reach the day when all of us can enjoy
in common Omar Khayyam's poetry in both
the Eastern and the Western form**

I once knew a man from Asia of the highest culture.
Educated at European universities during and after the
first World War, he was at the Great Divide in the evolution I have spoken of. He once told me how, in his early
youth, he lived with and loved *The Rubáiyát of Omar
Khayyam*. He thought he had made the original text 189

entirely his own, until he came to Britain and became acquainted with Fitzgerald's translation. Then, this in turn became – in the academic surroundings that began to transform him – his 'real' *Rubáiyát.**He returned home, however, and again found Omar Khayyam's poems such as he had once made them his own. The pendulum kept swinging, and, he concluded, 'even today I do not know which *Rubáiyát* is mine, Omar's or Fitzgerald's.'

The story needs no comment. Figuratively, there are still millions upon millions who do not know which *Rubáiyát* is theirs, Omar's or Fitzgerald's. We must reach the day when they, and all of us, can enjoy in common the *Rubáiyát* and the fact that we have it both in Omar's and in Fitzgerald's version.

*Rubáiyát is a verse form in Arabic, Persian and Turkish poetry, especially appreciated in classic Persian poetry with Omar Khayyam (1047–1122) as its most prominent representative.

The responsibility of the West
– and of the individual

**Ideas and ideologies of the West have become
factors of global significance**

*From address at The Rockefeller Institute, New York, 29 January
1959:*

In an often quoted statement, Arnold Toynbee has
pointed to the awareness of the responsibility of the
more highly developed societies for those who have
lagged behind in the race as the most characteristic new
fact of our generation. This new awareness, however,
seems to me to be rather a symptom of change than an
independent and decisive factor in the change. We can
easily trace its roots in the past and its background in
the present.

How much of this new awareness is spontaneous,
and how much of it is a response to a demand for a
share of the place in the sun by that vast majority of
mankind which has been left behind? Back of the demand and back of the response we find ideas that, in
national communities, broke through long ago in the
French Revolution, in the American Revolution and –
not to be forgotten – in the Soviet Revolution.

These ideologies of past and present generations
would not have brought our world to the ferment in
which we find it at present, had it not been for the development of communications over the last decades /.../

Likewise, difficult though it may be to envisage what

the standard of life and the political liberties in highly developed countries mean to such societies, the road has been opened to everyone in the most remote places of the globe to compare his position with that of more fortunate peoples. Thus, ideas and ideologies peculiar to the West have in our time, in their practical application, become factors in global development and of global significance.

The discoveries and inventions which have opened the doors for personal contacts all around the globe, and for the written and spoken word in every quarter, have, at the same time, put at our disposal means by which we have unprecedented possibilities to change conditions of life for the better, for all people. Our increased knowledge has given us new sources of power and new insight into the nature of disease. It may be that we are still far from mastering disease, and it may be that we are still far from mastering the new sources of energy sufficiently well to meet the demand of a quickly growing humanity for a life in dignity without fear. But, the newly developed perspectives are such that political economy need no longer be the 'dismal science' of the days of Malthus.

Thus, in this epoch of change we see science as a *primus motor* but likewise as a human activity from which we may expect many of the replies to our present-day problems as they are determined by our concepts of man and society in their new, world-wide application.

**The mistrust between man and man
has become existential. It is only within ourselves
that we can hope, by our own actions, to make a valid
contribution to a turn of the trend of events**

*Extract from the address »The Walls of Distrust« at Cambridge
University, 5 June 1958:*

It is easy to turn the responsibility over to others or, perhaps, to seek explanations in some kind of laws of history. It is less easy to look for the reasons within ourselves or in a field where we, all of us, carry a major responsibility. However, such a search is necessary, because finally it is only within ourselves and in such fields that we can hope, by our own actions, to make a valid contribution to a turn of the trend of events.

With your permission, I would in this context like to quote one of the influential thinkers of our time, whose personal history and national experience have given him a vantage point of significance.

In an address in Carnegie Hall in New York, in 1952, Martin Buber had the following to say:

'There have always been countless situations in which a man believes his life-interest demands that he suspect the other of making it his object to appear otherwise than he is... In our time something basically different has been added... One no longer merely fears that the other will voluntarily dissemble, but one takes it for granted that he cannot do otherwise... The other communicates to me the perspective that he has acquired on a certain subject, but I do not really take cognizance of his communication as knowledge. I do not take it seriously as a contribution to the information about this subject, but rather I listen for what drives the other to say what he says, for an unconscious motive… Since it is the idea of the other, it is for me an »ideology«. My main task in my intercourse with my fellowman becomes more and more… to see through and unmask him… With this changed basic attitude… the mistrust between man and man has become existential. This is so indeed in a double sense: It is first of all, no longer the uprightness, the honesty of the other which is in question, but the inner integrity of his existence itself… Nietzsche knew what he was doing when he praised the »art of mistrust«, and yet he did not know. For this game naturally only becomes complete as it becomes reciprocal… Hence one may foresee in the future a degree of reciprocity in existential mistrust where speech will turn into dumbness and sense into madness.'

I excuse myself for having quoted at such length from this speech. I have done so because out of the depth of his feelings Martin Buber has found expressions which it would be vain for me to try to improve.

Destructive forces represent, now as before, the greatest challenge man has to face

Scientists of genius, working here and in other research centers around the world, have made a unique contribution to progress, prosperity and peace. If their achievements have been turned to uses sometimes very far from their original intentions, it is not their fault. Nor is it the fault of their colleagues in the fields of theology, law, medicine, history and philosophy, or other branches of humane letters, if their contributions have not sufficed to create such psychological and political safeguards as would guarantee that the achievements of science be turned to man's benefit and not to his destruction.

But all of us, in whatever field of intellectual activity we work, influence to some degree the spiritual trend of our time. All of us may contribute to the breakdown of the walls of distrust and towards checking fatal tendencies in the direction of stale conformism and propaganda. How can this be done better or more effectively than by simple faithfulness to the independence of the spirit and to the right of the free man to free thinking and free expression of his thoughts? So, attitudes in line with the liberal traditions of this University emerge as a deeply significant element also in our efforts to master the political difficulties.

I have used strong words, but they reflect deep concern. For someone active primarily in the field of international politics it is today natural to appeal to the spirit for which Cambridge may be taken as a symbol. Deep-rooted conflicts which have run their course all through history, and seemed to reach a new culmination before and during the second World War, continue. And destructive forces which have always been with us make themselves felt in new forms. They represent, now as before, the greatest challenge man has to face.

At a press conference on 12 June 1958 Hammarskjöld repeated his »fear about the drift into what Buber has called existential reciprocal mistrust«. He criticized this despair of Western civilization which he found unjustified.

Freedom

**Freedom in the world of today is possible
only when the individual replaces outward
limitations on his freedom of action by self-imposed
laws of a mature conscience**

*From address at Johns Hopkins University, Baltimore, 14 June
1955:*

We hear much about freedom and the blessings of freedom. We hear less about the obligations of freedom and the ideals by which freedom must be guided. Every individual prefers freedom from constraint and freedom from intervention in his personal pursuit of happiness. But, as we all recognize, such freedom is possible in a world of order only when the individual replaces outward limitations on his freedom of action by self-imposed laws which may be, and frequently are, no less severe. An individualism carried to the extreme where you neither accept restraints imposed on you by society, or by your fellow men, nor submit yourself to the laws of a mature conscience, would lead to anarchy. This is true no less of international life than of life within your own country.

The attitude basic to international service places the pursuit of happiness under laws of conscience which alone can justify freedom. In accepting such a way of life we recognize the moral sovereignty of the responsible individual.

Loyalty

Loyalties to our fellow men are determined by ideals true to us

From address at Johns Hopkins University, 14 June 1955:

We are now ready to return to the question whether international service is possible without split loyalties in a divided world. The problem as posed here is to my mind unreal. We are true to this or that ideal, and this or that interest, because we have in openness and responsibility recognized it as an ideal and an interest true to us. We embrace ideals and interests in their own right, not because they are those of our environment or of this or that group. Our relations to our fellow men do not determine our attitude to ideals, but are determined by our ideals. If our attitude is consistent, we shall be consistent in our loyalties. If our attitude is confused, then our loyalties will also be divided.

In the world of today there is an urge to conformism which sometimes makes people complain of a lack of loyalty in those who criticize the attitudes prevalent in their environment. May I ask: who shows true loyalty to that environment, one who before his conscience has arrived at the conclusion that something is wrong and in all sincerity gives voice to his criticism, or the one who in self-protection closes his eyes to what is objectionable and shuts his lips on his criticism? The concept of loyalty is distorted when it is understood to mean blind acceptance. It is correctly interpreted when it is assumed to cover honest criticism.

Nobody should suffer for faithfulness to ideals of truth and justice provided he observes the laws of his country as well as the organization which he serves

The question to which I have just referred has attracted special attention in discussions concerning the attitude of those who work in international organizations, the policies in which in some cases may conflict with that of their home countries. Again I would say that the problem is unreal. The international civil servant who works for an organization with members of different ideologies and interests remains under the obligation that applies to all of us – to be faithful to truth as he understands it. In doing so he is loyal – both in relation to the organization and to his country. In doing so, he must, of course, subordinate himself to rules of good order, as all of us should do. Nobody should use his position in an international organization for attacks on his own country or its policies, however strongly he may feel that he is right. Nor should anybody, as a national, attack the international organization for which he is working, and thereby place himself outside the discipline and the procedure established for the maintenance of that organization. But it is equally true that nobody should suffer, either as a national, or in his position in the international organization, for faithfulness to ideals of truth and justice, provided he observes the laws of his country as well as of the organization which he serves. There cannot be, and there should not be, any real conflict between international service and international civil service, between the way of life we have been considering and the duties of someone engaged in professional work for the international community.

Maturity of mind

Intellectual honesty is the very key
to maturity of the mind

A central concept in Dag Hammarskjöld's speeches and private notes in »Markings« is what he describes as »the maturity of the mind«. In his radio statement 1954 he uttered the following about his religious convictions:

I feel that I can endorse those convictions without any compromise with the demands of that intellectual honesty which is the very key to maturity of mind.

A mature man's only form of support
is being faithful to his own convictions

In his inaugural address upon taking his seat as a member of the Swedish Academy, Stockholm, on 12 December 1954, Hammarskjöld talked about his predecessor, Hjalmar Hammarskjöld, his father:

A mature man is his own judge. In the end, his only form of support is being faithful to his own convictions. The advice of others may be welcome and valuable, but it does not free him from responsibility. Therefore, he may become very lonely. Therefore, too, he must run, with open eyes, the risk of being accused of obdurate self-sufficiency. As the war went on and difficulties increased, this was the fate of Hjalmar Hammarskjöld.

Hjalmar Hammarskjöld served as Prime Minister during the war years of 1914–1917 and became unpopular because of his strict and uncompromising policy of neutrality. In describing his father, Dag Hammarskjöld often seems to be describing himself, says Brian Urquhart in his biography of Hammarskjöld.

Respect for the word is the first commandment in the education to maturity

In a note in »Markings« 1954, Hammarskjöld wrote:

Respect for the word is the first requirement in the discipline through which a human being can be nurtured to maturity – intellectually, emotionally and morally.

Respect for the word – using it with strictest care and in uncompromising inner love of truth – is also for the society and the human race a condition for growth.

To misuse the word is to show contempt for man. It undermines the bridges and poisons the springs. In this way it leads us backward on the long road of human evolution.

The maturity of mind is evident to all as independence, courage and fairness in dealing with others

From address at Johns Hopkins University, 14 June 1955:

The dignity of man, as a justification for our faith in freedom, can be part of our living creed only if we revert to a view of life where maturity of mind counts for more than outward success and where happiness is no longer to be measured in quantitative terms. I doubt whether the author,* had he been given the chance to complete his work, would ever have found it possible to go far beyond this point, because the final reply is not one that can be given in writing, but only in terms of life. There is no formula to teach us how to arrive at maturity and there is no grammar for the language of inner life. His study, like the effort of every single individual, finally led him to the doorstep where the rest is silence because the rest is something that has to be resolved between a man and himself. The rest is silence – but the results of the inner dialogue are evident to all, evident as independence, courage and fairness in dealing with others, evident in true international service.

There is a maturity of mind required of those who give up rights and who aquire new rights in the vast venture of creating a true world community

In his address on the The Walls of Distrust at Cambridge University, 5 June 1958, he uttered:

There is a maturity of mind required of those who give up rights. There is a maturity of mind required of those who acquire new rights. Let us hope that, to an increasing extent, the necessary spiritual qualities will be shown on all sides.

The rights referred to the requirements demanded of the nations in establishing...

[...] an international democracy of peoples, bringing all nations – irrespective of history, size or wealth – together on an equal basis as partners in the vast venture of creating a true world community. But we have taken only the first steps, and they have often proved painful.

The ultimate fight is one between
the human and the sub-human

The conflict between different approaches to the liberty of man and mind or between different views of human dignity and the right of the individual is continuous. The dividing line goes within ourselves, within our own peoples and also within other nations. It does not coincide with any political or geographical boundaries. The ultimate fight is one between the human and the sub-human. We are on dangerous ground if we believe that any individual, any nation or any ideology has a monopoly on rightness, liberty and human dignity.

When we fully recognize this and translate our insight into words and action, we may also be able to re-establish full human contact and communications across geographical and political boundaries, and to get out of a public debate which often seems to be inspired more by a wish to impress than by a will to understand and to be understood.

*Russel W. Davenport, *The Dignity of Man*

Knowledge about man

**Our knowledge is too much concentrated
on techniques and we forget about man himself**

From address at Amherst College, Massachusetts, 13 June 1954:

We learn in order to know, and we wish to know in order to master, not other men, but the tools put in our hands for establishing a satisfactory life for ourselves and for all men. Too often our learning, our knowledge, and our mastery are too much concentrated on techniques and we forget about man himself. We may know a lot about the structure of the atom, or about the body of man, or about the organization of production or banking, without knowing much about the man whom the forces in the atom should serve, for whose body we find cures and for whose needs our productive and financial arrangements provide.

When I speak of knowledge in this context I do not mean the kind of knowledge which you can gain from textbooks, but the knowledge which you can derive only from a study of yourself and your fellow men, a study inspired by genuine interest and pursued with humility. The door to an understanding of the other party, with whom you may have to deal in business, in politics or in the international sphere, is a fuller understanding of yourself, since the other party, of course, is made fundamentally of the same stuff as you yourself.

Thus, no education is complete, in a world basically

united, which does not include man himself, and is not inspired by a recognition of the fact that you will not understand your enemy without understanding yourself, and that an understanding of your enemy will throw considerable light also on yourself and on your own motives /.../

In the United Nations our efforts would be useless, if it were not for that unity to which I have referred. And there would be no way forward, if it were not for the fact that greater insight is bound to lead to greater understanding and that greater understanding may open doors where previously there has seemed to be only a wall.

We need both men of faith and imagination and men of duty

From address at University of California, 13 May 1954:

For some people the driving force in life is faith in the success of their efforts. For others it is simply a sense of duty. We need both types of men. We need the man of faith and his imagination, his inspiration, in the search for great achievement. But we also need the other one, who is animated by his feeling of collective responsibility, without consideration of such recompense. We need both the architect and the bricklayer /.../

The founding fathers in San Francisco were the architects, the men of faith and imagination who wrote the Charter, tinder which the world community has a chance to develop from anarchy into order. Those in the Governments and Delegations, or in the Secretariat, who pursue the day-to-day operations, trying to meet emergencies as they arise, trying to explore possibilities and trying to give to the tools created by the Charter their maximum value, are the bricklayers who must devote themselves wholly to the effort regardless of any hopes of reaping any rewards of success.

I admit that for Governments and peoples, as for individuals serving the Organization, the experiences may sometimes be most frustrating. For example, who does not feel disappointed when a disagreement reflected in use of the veto prevents or delays a useful action which seems to be in the interest of all? But let us remember that such a disagreement is not the result of our efforts of cooperation. It is one of those conditions *in spite of which* and *against which* we must keep trying to develop cooperation /.../

The price of peace since 1945 has come high indeed and I would be the last to pretend that I can see any easy way out of continuing to pay that price for a long time to come. When I speak of the high price of peace, I am not thinking of the burden of armaments. That is in the picture, of course. But I am thinking primarily of the price in terms of the demands upon our capacity for patience and for steadiness of purpose. The process of learning to live together without war in this torn and distracted world of ours is going to continue to be painful and a constant challenge for the rest of our lives. Yet we know what the choice is. Either we manage it or we face disaster.

An echo of the music of the universe

**There is no man alone, because every man is a
microcosm and carries the whole world about him**

*Hammarskjöld was to speak briefly each year during the intermissions of the annual United Nations Day Concerts. From his first
UN Day Speech, 1953:*

The Charter of the United Nations, which was ratified
on October 24, 1945, makes the Organization a symbol
of ideas, and it should be recognized as an attempt to
translate into action a faith – the faith which once inspired a Beethoven in the Ninth Symphony to his great
profession of freedom, the brotherhood of man, and a
world of harmony. This is why music, and what only
music can express, may well have its honored place in
the celebration of United Nations Week.

In his Symphony of the World, Paul Hindemith has
tried to express in the universal language of music the
ancient belief in a basic harmony of the Universe. We
find this belief in old India, we meet it again in Greece,
we are familiar with its echoes in the writings of the
prophets of Israel. Let me quote here a later author
whose words seem to me to be a fitting comment on this
concert.

About 1635, Thomas Browne wrote in his *Religio
Medici:* »There is musick where ever there is harmony,
order, proportion: and thus far we may maintain the
musick of the Spheres; for those well ordered motions,

and regular paces, though they give no sound on to the ear yet to the understanding they strike a note most full of harmony.« In music »there is something of Divinity more than the ear discovers: it is an Hieroglyphical and shadowed lesson of the whole World, and creatures of God; such a melody to the ear as the whole World, well understood, would afford the understanding. In brief, it is a sensible fit of that harmony which intellectually sounds in the ears of God.«

These words yield their full meaning, reveal their human implications when we add to them this further quotation from Browne: »There is no man alone, because every man is a Microcosm, and carries the whole World about him.«

Starting with and in our own lives
the United Nations makes it possible for us all
to work for harmony in the world of man

In words that are no better than Browne's, but perhaps closer to our common language of today: Behind the simple harmonies of music, which may be grasped by our senses, we see dimly a greater harmony – a harmony of the whole World – that should resound also in the small world of man, in the limited sphere of our own life.

We are far from Browne's simple concept of the world. We may find it difficult to share his humble faith. But can we escape his conclusions? His is a hope for harmony in the world of men that should be valid for all times. The demand this hope places upon us may even

have a deeper significance for us than for our predecessors. There is no man alone. There is no escape from the duty to create harmony in that microcosm in which we, every one of us, are at the center. Whatever the development of the concepts of the Universe, whatever the changes in our faiths and creeds, our responsibility in this respect has certainly not decreased since the time when Browne wrote, or since the old days when the first dreams about a world of harmony took shape in the East.

Thus, an old philosophy of the Universe and the music which it has inspired, and to which we have listened, are linked to essential elements in our own personal lives – but likewise in our lives as men and women responsible to our neighbours, to society, and to history.

It is not presumptuous to say that those elements are present in the background also of the work which is carried on – or should be carried on – in and by the United Nations. In our preoccupation with the outward forms, the established procedures, the publicity, and the immediate issues which attract our attention from day to day, we may tend to forget that at the very basis of this Organization there is the will of all peoples to create a world of harmony. The United Nations in its fundamental purpose is one of the means by which it is possible for all of us, starting with and in our own lives, to work for that harmony in the world of man which our forefathers were striving for as an echo of the music of the Universe.

A confession of faith in the victorious human spirit

This statement on 24 October 1960 was the last of the statements made by dag Hammarskjöld at the annual observation of United

Nations Day. It was recorded at the time and repeated eleven months later during the memorial ceremony in the General Assembly Hall for him and those who had died with him on 18 September 1961. The Philadelphia Orchestra returned to play again on this occasion Beethoven's Ninth Symphony.

It is the tradition that the Organization marks United Nations Day with a concert including the final movement of Beethoven's Ninth Symphony. Today we shall, for the first time in this hall, listen to the symphony in its entirety.

It is difficult to say anything, knowing that the words spoken will be followed by this enormous confession of faith in the victorious human spirit and in human brotherhood, a confession valid for all times and with a depth and wealth of expression never surpassed. However, this concert is in celebration of United Nations Day and it has been felt that a few words may remind us of the purpose for which we have assembled.

When the Ninth Symphony opens we enter a drama full of harsh conflict and dark threats. But the composer leads us on, and in the beginning of the last movement we hear again the various themes repeated, now as a bridge towards a final synthesis. A moment of silence and a new theme is introduced, the theme of reconciliation and joy in reconciliation. A human voice is raised in rejection of all that has preceded and we enter the dreamt kingdom of peace. New voices join the first and mix in a jubilant assertion of life and all that it gives us when we meet it, joined in faith and human solidarity.

On his road from conflict and emotion to reconciliation in this final hymn of praise, Beethoven has given us a confession and a credo which we, who work within and for this Organization, may well make our own. We take part in the continuous fight between conflicting interests and ideologies which so far has marked the history of mankind, but we may never lose our faith that the first movements one day will be followed by the fourth movement. In that faith we strive to bring order and purity into chaos and anarchy. Inspired by that faith we try to impose the laws of the human mind and of the integrity of the human will on the dramatic evolution in which we are all engaged and in which we all carry our resonsibility.

The road of Beethoven in his Ninth Symphony is also the road followed by the authors of the Premble of the Charter. It begins with the recognition of the threat under which we all live, speaking as it does of the need to save succeeding generations from the scourge of war which has brought untold sorrow to mankind. It moves on to a reaffirmation of faith in the dignity and worth of the human person. And it ends with the promise to practice tolerance and live together in peace with one another as good neighbours and to unite our strength to maintain peace.

This year, the fifteenth in the life of the Organization, is putting it to new tests. Experience has shown how far we are from the end which inspired the Charter. We are indeed still in the first movements. But no matter how deep the shadows may be, how sharp the conflicts, how tense the mistrust reflected in what is said and done in our world today as reflected in this hall and in this house, we are not permitted to forget that we have too much in common, too great a sharing of interests and too much that we might lose together, for ourselves and for succeeding generations, ever to weaken in our efforts to surmount the difficulties and not to turn the simple human values, which are our common heritage, into the firm foundation on which we may unite our strength and live together in peace.

May this be enough as a reminder of the significance of this day. And may now the symphony develop its themes, uniting us in its recognition of fear and its confession of faith.

On modern art

**The art of the past aimed at a tranfiguration
of reality while modern art strives for an explanation
and re-creation of reality**

*Hammarskjöld's great interest in modern art led to close contacts
with New York's Museum of Modern Art. A succession of paintings chosen by him were loaned by the museum for the walls of his
office suite and private dining room on the thirty-eighth floor of
the Secretariat building. Ten years after he gave this speech it was
extensively quoted by Rene d'Harnoncourt, director of the museum, in a statement given at the unveiling ceremony of Barbara
Hepworth's sculpture, »Single Form«, in front of the UN Secretariat
building on June 11, 1964, a project initiated by Hammarskjöld
and brought to fruition after his death under U Thant. From his
speech at the Museum of Modern Art, 19 October 1954:*

The art collected here is not modern in the sense that it
has the vain ambition of expressing the latest of the
shifting fashions of a mass civilization which long ago
lost its anchorage in a firm scale of values, inspired by a
generally accepted faith. Nor is it modern in the sense of
the comic strips or similar attempts to use the techniques of art to cater for broad emotional needs through
a cheap representation of a sentimentalized reality. It is
a museum for »modern art« – that is, for you and for
me, a museum for the art which reflects the inner problems of our generation and is created in the hope of
meeting some of its basic needs /…/

If we demand of art that it should be the expression of

a mature and balanced mastery of the relationship of man and his civilization to life, then modern art, to be sure, does not reach levels that were already achieved in a distant past in our Western civilization. No – then it is not progress.

However that may be, there are two qualities which are shared by modern art and the scientific sphere. One is the courage of an unprejudiced search for the basic elements of experience. The other one is perseverance in the fight for mastery of those elements.

The need for the courage of search establishes a decisive difference between modern art and the art of the past, living in and expressing a world of faith. Agnostic search, based on a re-evaluation of all values, is a quality of modern art that is an essential expression of the spiritual situation of our generation. But this quality, in itself, must prevent modern art from achieving the kind of perfection which we meet in the Cathedral of Chartres or in the paintings of Giotto.

The second quality – perseverance in the fight for mastery – is on the contrary the main great quality that modern art shares with the art of the past. I have already quoted Malraux. Let me quote him again: The victory of an artist over his servitude joins the victory of art itself over the fate of man. The romantic conviction expressed in these words is what makes Piero della Francesca and Rembrandt, Cezanne and Braque, members of one great fraternity. In that conviction, and in the fight it inspires, the artists who aimed at a transfiguration of reality meet the artists who now strive for an explanation and re-creation of reality.

**Modern art teaches us to see by forcing us to
use our senses, our intellect and our sensibility
to follow its road of exploration**

In its search for the basic elements of the world surrounding us and in its fight for mastery of these elements, modern art has revealed to us also where lies the
real victory of the great artists of the past. Without making us eclectics, it has helped us to understand – as far as
that is possible without sharing the atmosphere of faith
in which they were born – what has been achieved in the
harmony of the best works of the past. Modern art has
forged keys to a perfection which it has not itself reached.
Shouldering courageously the problems of modern
man, reflecting his situation in a world of conflicts born
out of his own achievements, it has, thus, earned, the
recompense of being permitted also to illuminate the
greatness of man in the high artistic achievements of the
past.

Art gives more to life than it takes from it. True art
does not depend on the reality about which it tells. Its
message lies in the new reality which it creates by the
way in which it reflects experience. In our minds, all of
us, sometimes chisel beauty out of the stone of matter. If
we had the courage and perseverance to push these experiences of a few moments to their extreme point, we
would share in the effort of the modern artist to isolate
beauty from the impurity of life, even if it has to be at
the cost of dissolving the very forms of life. Why then,
seeing modern art, should we feel estranged when we do
not at the first glance recognize the familiar aspects of
our everyday world?

Modern art teaches us to see by forcing us to use our senses, our intellect and our sensibility to follow it on its road of exploration. It makes us seers – seers like Ezra Pound when, in the first of his Pisan Cantos, he senses »the enormous tragedy of the dream in the peasant's bent shoulders.« Seers – and explorers – these we must be if we are to prevail.

The camera taught me to see

Camera images must not be allowed to replace the use of our eyes

Excerpt from an article in Swedish Foto *magazine, number 12, 1958:*

For most who have developed a serious interest in photography, it is seen as a means, with all the richness of association a picture can offer, of retaining memories of people, places and events. In striving to do this satisfactorily, we are not averse to the desire, on this modest level, to reach a kind of self-fulfilment, both technical and aesthetic.

However distant in various ways the actual picture is from what deserves to be called art, the dedicated photographer is spurred in his work by motives not dissimilar to those familiar to the creative artist. I believe that among the multitude who currently use a camera, far more than one would guess do harbour such a secret ambition – even though we have all often encountered those for whom photography appears to be a nervous habit and who fire off picture after picture, almost as a substitute for the use of their eyes.

It is better to teach oneself to see than to have one's visualization provided by others

When photography becomes a real hobby, the camera becomes a means to learn to see in pictures, but also to see and memorise the play of lines, the distribution of light, the balance between detail and the whole.

Looking back on the results of my perennially active interest in photography – my own and others' – what has been meaningful is far less the pictures I have taken, in the periods when I was able to cultivate my interest, than what I learned in 'seeing'. And it is better to learn to see than to have one's view decided by others: however inferior our own products may seem compared to what others achieve, in the final analysis we learn more from our own than any number of pictures by the true artists of the camera, however great our debt of gratitude for their guidance.

Technically questionable pictures can be 'real' when they are bearers of the atmosphere of an experience

One evening when, at the request of an editor, I was leafing through some older pictures, it became clear to me that there was none among them I could call a 'best picture' or even a really good one. Too many criteria compete for the expressions to have much meaning.

One of the pictures was a portrait that, through a combination of circumstances, recreated a situation in which a person had been harmoniously incorporated, not as central object but more as the bearer of an atmosphere. Is such a portrait photographically good or not?

Another was an evening scene of a thundercloud over the plain around Chartres. Technically it is questionable and yet the photograph is 'real' because it shows the 222 play of forces around the cathedral which, its massive-ness in human measurement notwithstanding, diminishes to a minor detail in the shadow of the cloud.

Another was a travel picture showing a poor Burmese woman at prayer before a reclining Buddha while her daughter impatiently follows the photographer's play.

Another was a picture of a defoliated oak branch with a play of lines reflecting the balance between power and nervous sensibility so often evidenced in nature's own creations.

Another was a picture of a path along the Abiskojokk River in northern Sweden, perhaps divulging its message only to the observer for whom the characteristic play of light over the landscape reflects a personal experience of such a timeless world at rest.

Again: what is the photographic value of these pictures? I remain dubious, and yet they all show in their way why photography as a hobby has given me so much that even in the busiest of periods I try to find a way to cleave to it.

A room of quiet

**A place where doors may open
to the indefinite lands of thought and prayer**

*Dag Hammarskjöld personally planned and supervised in every
detail the creation of the United Nations Meditation Room as it
exists today. It is located off the public lobby of the General
Assembly Hall. He wrote the following text of the leaflet which is
given to the thousands who visit this room, in 1957, when the
room was reopened to the public. The fresco on the front wall to
which he refers is the work of the noted Swedish artist and his
friend, Bo Beskow. The block of iron ore in the middle of the room
is also Swedish.*

We all have within us a center of stillness surrounded by
silence.

This house, dedicated to work and debate in the service of peace, should have one room dedicated to silence
in the outward sense and stillness in the inner sense.

It has been the aim to create in this small room a place
where the doors may be open to the infinite lands of
thought and prayer.

People of many faiths will meet here, and for that reason none of the symbols to which we are accustomed in
our meditation could be used.

However, there are simple things which speak to us
all with the same language. We have sought for such
things and we belive that we have found them in he shaft
of light striking the shimmering surface of solid rock.

So, in the middle of the room we see a symbol of how,

daily, the light of the skies gives life to the earth on which we stand, a symbol to many of us of how the light of the spirit gives life to matter.

**It is for those who come here
to fill the void with what they find
in their center of stillness**

But the stone in the middle of the room has more to tell us. We may see it as an altar, empty not because there is no God, not because it is an altar to an unknown god, but because it is dedicated to the God whom man worships under many names and in many forms.

The stone in the middle of the room reminds us also of the firm and permanent in a world of movement and change. The block of iron ore has the weight and solidity of the everlasting. It is a reminder of that cornerstone of endurance and faith on which all human endeavor must be based.

The material of the stone leads our thoughts to the necessity for choice between destruction and construction, between war and peace. Of iron man has forged his swords, of iron he has also made his ploughshares. Of iron he has constructed tanks, but of iron he has likewise bulit homes for man. The block of iron ore is part of wealth we have inherited on this earth of ours. How are we to use it?

The shaft of light strikes the stone in a room of utter simplicity. There are no other symbols, there is nothing to distract our attention or to break in on the stillness within ourselves. When our eyes travel from these symbols to the front wall they meet a simple pattern opening up the room to the harmony, freedom and balance of space.

There is an ancient saying that the sense of a vessel is not in its shell but in the void. So it is with this room. It is for those who come here to fill the void with what they find in their center of stillness.

Linnaeus – the continuity of spiritual life

New generations in the Western world have broken out of the sets of problems to which »une littérature engagée« seeks the answers

Dag Hammarskjöld was a great admirer of Linnaeus, »a shining prince of the land of summer«, as he called him in his Presidential address at the celebration of the 250th anniversary of the birth of Linnaeus in the Swedish Academy in Stockholm, 20 December 1957. Linnaeus and Hammarskjöld shared a love of Swedish nature as well as a sensibility for the Swedish language. As »matter-of-fact poetry«, Hammarskjöld characterized Linnaeus' descriptions of the Swedish land, thereby characterizing his own style of lyrical precision.

This extract from Hammarskjöld's Presidential address deals with the position of the writer in a time of growing material progress.

The relationship of a nation – and a generation – to older literature tells something about the continuity of spiritual life. It can also give an idea about the conditions of writing and of the writer: what is the reader seeking, and why? /.../

Perhaps this might also narrow the gap to the immediately preceding generation of writers, a gap which, now as always, is threatening because of the illusion that the old order is dead as all is renewed.

There is one possible reason for the estrangement from the past that is disquieting. In a mass culture, where publicity, working in the interest of sales, is constantly harping on the idea that the latest must be the best, the book, in the view of many, becomes relegated to the ranks of disposable and rapidly aging consumer goods. This may lead to an industrialization of literature, which pays attention to the indications about public taste in the best-seller lists in preference to that which is essential and therefore vital. In a situation which for such reasons, and perhaps also for other and deeper ones, is characterized by the quest for novelty and by conformism, a weakening of the position of older literature would be natural. The risk is enhanced if at the same time the position of the written word as such is becoming more precarious.

The book now has to compete with the press, and jointly they must hold their own against new forms of expression and communication: the films, radio and television. The need for personal contact with literature of quality reflects an acquired taste. A form of expression requiring less activity on the part of the recipient is favoured by that law of least resistance which prevails in this as in other fields.

In the end, we are faced here by the question of the intellectual climate and what determines it. It would be presumptuous to try, here and now, to contribute to this discussion. It is a banality which need not be further developed in this connection, to say that the present has given unusual weight to material progress, and that this means that it has deflected interest from spiritual exercises and found ways of satisfying it by a thousand and one new inventions. Nor is it an original view – whatever importance it may have – that new generations in the Western world have broken out of the sets of problems 230 to which *une littérature engagée* seeks the answers.

**A risk of literature changing into reporting aimed at
filling the mental vacuum of increasing leisure
without worry or effort for the reader**

Observers of the international currents of today may be
tempted to name another tendency, although so far it
has not made a very deep imprint in our country. It may
be that the cult of amorphous spontaneity in art and of a
philosophy of absurdity which is calling the tune in
some quarters these days, will prove to be a transitory
phenomenon. No matter what new paths it may open
for creative writing, it contains risks of a growing estrangement from readers whose interest is a prerequisite
for the continued life of a work of art.

Eliot has spoken of our era as one when wisdom has
been forgotten for knowledge and knowledge for information. May we escape a situation where these words
become more than an expression of frustration, and
where beside an esoteric poetry – which will probably
always have its practitioners – there is produced nothing but literature where realism has been changed into
reporting aimed at filling the mental vacuum of increasing leisure without worry or effort for the reader.

In such a situation the dead writers would become
definitely forgotten. To keep their works alive is also a
means of making room for new, creative writing which,
like that of their precursors, is begotten in earnest and
often born in pain.

The mental climate here referred to is also influenced,
and perhaps not least, by political factors. One of these
deserves mention here. This generation has seen Europe
lose much of the powerful position it occupied for cen-

turies, and a wave of nationalism has swept the continents. The revolutionary events we witness have led many into a defeatism which, although unspoken, is revealed by its inseparable companions: fatigue, bitterness and sterile self-assertion. In this development, there are traces of the life of nations in earlier periods of upsetting social change – however difficult it may sometimes be to recognize in the coexistence of nations the principles for which one has once fought in one's own country.

There are good reasons, and good chances, to offer resistance to such a situation. The old is not so rotten, nor the new so immature as many seem to think.

What Europe has lost in power
can be made up by leadership

In spite of the changes in its external position, Europe is certainly able, in these various contexts, to keep a place worthy of its traditions. What has been lost in power can be made up by leadership. One condition is that Europe understands how to develop and maintain the values which are the foundation of her spiritual greatness. In this, every nation has its role to play. This Academy has part of the responsibility for the way in which Sweden meets the demands placed on her.

When Linnaeus, after his years abroad, was tempted by most favourable offers to remain there, he declined them because 'a higher urge pulled him towards his Fatherland'. Sweden to Linnaeus was the country where he wished to round out his life's work. It was done as he willed it. The scholar, however, knew no national frontiers. He was a European and, as a European, a citizen of the world. Much has changed, but it is still possible to balance and reconcile home and world, heritage and task in this manner. This can provide an answer to even larger problems than those of the individual.

A new look at the Himalayas

**On the top of the hill the stupa dreamed its dream
of a world beyond pain and vicissitude**

*After a visit to Nepal in March 1959 Hammarskjöld wrote an
article for the National Geographic magazine, »A New Look at
Everest«, to accompany some very beautiful photographs he had
taken from an airplane of Everest, Annapurna and other Himalayan peaks. He also visited some holy places. These experiences
made a great impact, reflected in the article, which is rendered
unabriged.*

We flew north from Calcutta to Kathmandu in the early
afternoon. The season was beginning to change, and
heavy clouds had already condensed over the mountains.

I was sitting in the cockpit with the pilot – a man as
able as he was pleasant – and he told me eloquently
about what I did not see. He spoke with glowing enthusiasm about his flights into the Himalayas, during
which he found a sense of freedom and elation that gave
him the best moments of his life.

After a reception in Kathmandu, a representative of
the government, knowing of my interest in mountaineering, asked me whether I would like to fly into the
eastern ranges of the Himalayas early the next morning
before the start of official discussions that had brought
me to Nepal. The King would put at our disposal his
plane and pilot, the same young Sikh who had flown us
from Calcutta.

I accepted eagerly. From then on I kept my fingers crossed, hoping that the weather would make its contribution to what promised to be a unique experience snatched from work in a couple of morning hours.

In the late evening we went strolling through the old city. The moon was bright, and over the narrow streets, lying in dark shadow, the roofs with their stern but festive architecture glimmered in the light.

It was the time when people went to bed. The shops were closing, and the street vendors, who had spent the afternoon selling and buying before their charcoal fires and spinning their long tales, were going home. Finally, we drifted practically alone among the temples and palaces with their fantastic multicolored wooden carvings, which seemed to come to life in the shimmering light.

Our Nepalese friend and guide suggested a visit to the great Buddhist shrine of Swayambhunath on a hill outside the city. Although it was late, I accepted, as I knew that the rest of our time would be mostly taken up by work. I did so not only because of my wish to see this famous place, but also because I hoped that in the clear moonlight we might get a view over the foothills toward the mountains.

We went as far as the car would take us. Then we walked the narrow, circular road up the steep hill on the top of which the stupa dreamed its dream of a world beyond pain and vicissitude in the shadow of the timeless mountains.

**The mountains are holy to the people as
the dwelling of the gods and for that reason
they should be approached in the spirit of reverence**

The air had the freshness of a spring night at Easter time in Burgundy. The association may seem farfetched, but the hills around led my thoughts to the land about Vézelay, where a shrine rises in the same way as a goal of pilgrimage.

The stillness was broken by chattering screams and noises, and soon we were surrounded by monkeys, surprised but seemingly also pleased to get this unexpected company at a late hour.

Two Tibetan monks in their high boots were walking around the stupa, turning the prayer wheels as they passed.* At the side open toward Kathmandu we stopped and looked out over the wide valley. A few lights still shone in the city and in Patan. For the rest, everything was asleep in a quiet that seemed to be in deep harmony with the spirit to which the shrine was dedicated. We were not far from the birthplace of the Buddha, and back of us the stupa rose against the night sky in a silence broken only by the light metallic sounds from the prayer wheels.

One of the monks opened the screen doors to a side chapel in which a big Buddha could barely be seen. Silently the monk invited us in and gave us candles and flowers. To share with him his reverence for the mystery of life was easy in this setting, so intensely reflecting the endlessness of man's search and the greatness of the world to which he belongs.

The clouds had disappeared, but a haze had arisen in

the cool night and cut us off from the view of the high mountains. Although they were invisible, we could nonetheless strongly feel their presence in the deep blue behind the foothills.

I have described this evening because it gave me such a perfect introduction to our flight the next morning into the mountains. They are holy to the people as the dwelling of the gods, and for that reason they should be approached in the spirit into which our visit to the stupa had initiated us.

I learned later that because of this reverence for the mountains – but naturally also for more secular reasons – the government heretofore had permitted only a few persons to photograph the high ranges from the air.

*Worship of stupa consist in walking around the monument in the direction taken by the path of the sun.

The icy wastes of the Himalayas were a world far beyond human comprehension

After sunrise the next morning, the haze had gone and the sky was without a cloud. When we came down to the airstrip, the icy summits of the closest mountains stood out sharply over the green hills around the valley.

We flew through the valleys in the direction of Gauri Sankar and Everest. Even if we had never come to these mountains, it would have been a great experience just to see the beauty of the valleys and of the hillsides in the early morning light, the structure of the landscape, and the picturesque way in which cultivation and villages 238 have developed.

The plane in which we were flying was a DC-3, non-pressurized and without oxygen. That naturally set an altitude limit for the flight; we flew at a height of twelve to fifteen thousand feet.

Our route took us first in under the overwhelming south wall of Gauri Sankar, with its beautiful double summit consecrated to the two Hindu deities that give the mountain its name. At our altitude we seemed to approach it at mid-height. Its vast size gave the impression that we were even closer to the mountainside than we were.

A somewhat lighthearted association was that this must be the way a fly feels as it approaches a house where it hopes to sit down on the wall for a nice quiet rest in the sun. Then, as we came closer, my climber's instincts were aroused and I started speculating – in vain – on possible routes of access for those who one day might brave this most inaccessible south mountain wall.

But planes move fast, and a few minutes later we had, so to speak, rounded a corner and were looking in over the icy wastes of the Himalayas. Forbidding in its bold, sculptural structure, it was a world far beyond human comprehension and of the harsh purity we are accustomed to find in the miniature world of crystals. But here it met the eye in proportions that reduced our human world to a microcosm.

**Many have failed and their glory, written in the
history of the mountains, is that they went to
the limits of the humanly possible and were defeated
by circumstances beyond human mastery**

Swinging southeast, we left these areas behind us and
headed toward Everest. Over the highest green hills,
which seemed to be clad in dark green moss, the Everest
range stretched out in compact strength. The pilot
pointed to a sharp peak behind the nearest ice-clad
mountains. It wore a plume of snow, made by strong
northwesterly winds. This was Everest, its special rank
and position marked with a truly regal ornament.

From here on the route became somewhat confusing
to me. The pilot found his way through valleys, over
passes, and between mountains with an impressive
familiarity that left me far behind in my effort to orient
myself. It added to my confusion that I developed a kind
of hunting fever with my camera; I felt I must try to get a
chronicle in pictures of the constantly changing views
and renewed experiences of stunning beauty.

Mount Everest? Is it heresy to say that it somewhat let
me down? Beautiful in its clean outlines? Yes, both that
and impressive. But it stood, from the angle at which we
saw it, without that accent which separates one mountain from another and gives it a personality to stamp its
mark on your mind.

Now I ranged Everest in the files of my memory in
very much the same way as I could Mont Blanc –
a mountain singled out by its proportions and by its history in human terms more than by other qualities.
240 I thought of Hillary's gaunt stride and ruddy face, I

remembered Tenzing's soft handshake and subtle smile.

Superficially, they were an oddly matched pair, but combining qualities that brought them to that summit we saw in front of us. There, expressing an attitude I have often met in the fraternity to which they belong, they displayed the flags not only of their countries but also of the United Nations.

However, while thinking of those who had succeeded, I could not forget those who had failed. They have been many, and their glory, written into the history of the mountain, is that they went to the limits of the humanly possible and were defeated only by circumstances beyond human mastery.

The sleeping Hindu god and the silent Buddhist monks crystallized two of the great spiritual currents that have grown out of the meeting between man and the mountains

The first hour had flown away. It was necessary to return if we were to be back in time, and if we wished to avoid the assembling clouds. We came back to Gauri Sankar, and I decided to try to get a full picture of the south wall.

On my first attempt, I felt that I did not succeed, and, forgetting the situation, I asked the pilot to make a second round under the mountain. This time I succeeded. ... Meanwhile, however, we had lost altitude, and I could not help smiling – perhaps a little apprehensively – when I saw the pilot looking down through a side window to judge if he would get safely over the range we had to pass.

The experiences of this first contact with the Himalayas from the air were such that I asked the authorities if, on our flight to Delhi somewhat later, we could follow the high mountains west of Kathmandu for a distance, in order to cover at least Annapurna. In their generous hospitality, they at once agreed.

During short visits to a country for professional purposes, there is little time for sightseeing. Before we left Kathmandu, however, I had another experience that, in its way, tied together the first visit to the Himalayas and what we were to see the next time. Linking the two flights, it also created a bridge to the night at Swayambhunath. Again, it was a visit made with friends, and on a moonlit night.

Just outside the city lies a meadow surrounded by high trees but with a view across the valley to Swayambhunath. It is called the Twenty-two Fountains, for just where a steep hillside breaks the plain, there is a long stone ramp through which the cold waters of a mountain stream burst forth in many openings. It is a place steeped in the atmosphere of the mountains and yet stamped with the mark of ancient, high civilization, as sure in its artistic sense as in its sense of how to create a harmonious interplay between the work of men and the surrounding landscape.

At the side of the ramp lies a small square pond built of stone, eroded by water and frost. Down into it lead worn steps. Resting in the pond lies a statue of the sleeping Vishnu, sunk so deep in the water that only the upper parts of the body break the surface.

The moonlight played on the wet figure, contrasting
242 with the red glow from fires burning a short distance from

where we stood. The silence was of the kind that is to be found only in the mountains, a silence that is audible.

The charcoal fires were burning at a rest site on one of the roads from the north. Round them were grouped pilgrims on their way to Swayambhunath, preparing their evening food without a word and without a glance at the strangers who passed.

The sleeping Hindu god and the silent Buddhist monks crystallized two of the great spiritual currents that have grown out of the meeting between man and the mountains. They were of the mountains and of one spirit with the mountains. But they fused into the scenery the soul and the human perspective without which our feeling for nature is sterile and empty aestheticism.

**Annapurna's beauty of structure and her majesty,
far surpassing that of Everest, seemed a Potala*,
built by the gods for their incarnation**

The morning of our flight to Delhi was perfect. The route took us first straight toward Tibet. Over the broad pass we could look from a great distance onto the high Tibetan plateau. Then we were in the mountains again, but with a great change of atmosphere. Here the peaks seemed to be isolated giants, each with its own personality.

The first new shock was the Machhapuchhare (the Fish's Tail), a Matterhorn in its bold, towering greatness and its pure balance of lines up to the sharp summit. But soon this impression was surpassed by another.

Climbing in a half circle over a lower range, we suddenly had before us Annapurna, with a beauty of struc-   243 ture and a majesty far surpassing that of Everest or Gauri Sankar. It seemed a Potala, built by the gods for their incarnation not as frail human beings but as giants. The contrast between the sovereign quiet of the mountaintop and the wild ranges leading in toward it added to the otherworldliness, the feeling that we had penetrated into a world of cosmic purpose and character.

In spite of his long experience, the pilot was plainly moved by the sight. If it is possible in an airplane to simulate a tender stroke of affection, that is what he did, using the plane as his fingertips when rounding the glaciers and the rocks.

So we reached the final point, Dhaulagiri, a brutal mass, uninviting with its steep fields of ice and snow furrowed by innumerable ravines, as forbidding as a clenched fist. It is indeed appropriate that this is one of the latest of major Himalayan peaks to be conquered by man. A six-man Swiss team reached the top on May 13, 1960.

To someone who has learned to love the mountains and see in mountaineering one of the most satisfactory ways we can test our ability against nature – yet basically as a tribute to nature – it is somewhat shameful to approach the Himalayas by plane. My last words here should be a tribute to our pilot, who did his job with the deep insight and love of the mountains that characterize the true mountaineer. He managed to convey, at least to this passenger, a bit of the feeling of liberty, strength, and harmony we achieve when we fight a mountain and live with it, helped only by our body and our mind.

*Potala is the name of the palace in Lhasa, Tibet, built in the 17th century as seat of the Dalai Lama.

Last words to the staff

**A truly independent international Secretariat
may develop as an instrument for the preservation
of peace and security of increasing significance**

*From Dag Hammarskjöld's last speech, which was made to the
Secretariat staff on the occasion of Staff Day in the General Assembly Hall, 8 September 1961:*

The general world situation and its repercussions on the Organization have unavoidably left their mark on the Secretariat. In particular the discussions in the last session of the General Assembly have raised far-reaching questions on the nature of the Secretariat. What is at stake is a basic question of principle: Is the Secretariat to develop as an international Secretariat, with the full independence contemplated in Article 100 of the Charter, or is it to be looked upon as an inter-governmental – not international – Secretariat, providing merely the necessary administrative services for a conference machinery? This is a basic question and the answer to it affects not only the working of the Secretariat but the whole of the future of international relations.

If the Secretariat is regarded as truly international, and its individual members as owing no allegiance to any national government, then the Secretariat may develop as an instrument for the preservation or peace and security of increasing significance and responsibilities. If a contrary view were to be taken, the Secretariat itself would not be available to Member governments as an instrument, additional to the normal diplomatic methods, for active and growing service in the common interest.

Our task is an essential work for building dams against the floods of disintegration and violence

In a situation like the one now facing all peoples of the world, as represented in this Organization, it is understandable that staff members should sometimes feel frustrated and even depressed. In that they are not different from their fellow beings in other positions influenced by the trend of world events. There is only one answer to the human problem involved, and that is for all to maintain their professional pride, their sense of purpose, and their confidence in the higher destiny of the Organization itself, by keeping to the highest standards of personal integrity in their conduct as international civil servants and in the quality of the work that they turn out on behalf of the Organization. This is the way to defend what they believe in and to strengthen this Organization as an instrument of peace for which they wish to work. Dejection and despair lead to defeatism – and defeat.

It is true that we are passing through a period of unusual threats to human society and to peace. The dangers are too well known for me to add any comments here. If anything, you hear and see too much about them in the headlines of every paper. It is also true that the role of the Organization is necessarily a modest one, subordinated as it must be to governments, and through governments to the will of the peoples.

But, although the dangers may be great and although our role may be modest, we can feel that the work of the Organization is *the* means through which we all, jointly, can work so as to reduce the dangers. It would be too dramatic to talk about our task as one of waging a war for peace, but it is quite realistic to look at it as an essential and – within its limits – effective work for building dams against the floods of disintegration and violence.

Let us work in the conviction that our work has a meaning beyond the narrow individual one and has meant something for man

Those who serve the Organization can take pride in what it has done already in many, many cases. I know what I am talking about if I say, for example, that short of the heavy work in which each of you has had his or her part, the Congo would by now have been torn to pieces in a fight which in all likelihood would not have been limited to that territory, but spread far around, involving directly or indirectly many or all of the countries from which you come. I also know what the activities of the Organization in the economic and social fields have meant for the betterment of life of millions, and for the creation of a basis for a happier future.

This is not said in a spirit of boastful satisfaction with what this Organization has been able to do – which, alas, falls far short of the needs – but as a realistic evaluation of the contribution we all of us, individually, have been permitted to make through our work for this Organization. It is false pride to register and to boast to the world about the importance of one's work, but it is false humility, and finally just as destructive, not to recognize – and recognize with gratitude – that one's work has a sense. Let us avoid the second fallacy as carefully as the first, and let us work in the conviction that our work *has* a meaning beyond the narrow individual one and *has* meant something for man.

Epilogue

From the chapter entitled »Final mission to the Congo« in the book »Public Papers of the Secretaries-General of the United Nations, Volume 5, Dag Hammarskjöld 1960–1961«. The text below was written by Andrew Cordier and Wilder Foote:

Hammarskjöld had decided to go to Leopoldville before the opening on September 19 of the sixteenth annual session of the General Assembly. One purpose was a personal effort to persuade Tshombe to a reconciliation with Adoula and thus bring a peaceful end to the secession of Katanga and provide the central government of the Congo with the strongest and widest political base it had enjoyed since independence. Hammarskjöld also intended to explore with Adoula possibilities for progressive reductions in the scope of UN participation in civil administration and in the size and expense of the UN Congo Force.

It was announced that he would leave on September 12, arriving in Leopoldville the next day, and plan to return to Headquarters on September 18, just in time for the beginning of the Assembly session.

During the last few days before he left Headquarters the Secretary-General had been pressed by his principal lieutenants in the Congo to authorize forceful measures of one kind or another to complete the evacuation of the remaining foreign officers and mercenaries and to cope with the growing threat of violence by the ultras against the UN forces and civilian personnel in Katanga. Hammarskjöld's inclination, as he cabled to Linnér, was »to remain strong but to sit tight and to let the medicine do its work without, if possible, new injections.« As the situation in Elisabethville grew more ominous just before his departure he indicated approval, in principle and as a last resort, of a plan for repeating the steps taken on August 28 if further efforts to persuade Tshombe to cooperate failed. However, he thought Linnér and the others understood that no major action should be launched before consulting him after his arrival during the afternoon of September 13 at Leopoldville.

His lieutenants, however, went ahead early in the morning of that day, apparently on the assumption that they could repeat in a couple of hours and without bloodshed the successful surprise operation of August 28, thus dealing a crippling and probably decisive blow to the Katanga independence movement. This time, however the gendarmerie and armed ultras drawn from the white population of Elisabethville were ready. The UN troop units immediately came under fire and sporadic fighting and sniping in and around Elisabethville continued through the day. Tshombe, after first offering to arrange a cease-fire, disappeared from his home and could not be located. There were mercenary-led attacks on UN troops in Kamina, Jadotville and Albertville. A single Fouga Magister jet fighter, flown by a mercenary pilot, bombed and strafed UN troop positions and transport planes. Since the United Nations did not have a single military aircraft it dominated the skies.

O'Brien compounded the difficulties by announcing
to correspondents in Elisabethville during the day that

»the secession of Katanga is ended,« thus reinforcing the impression that the United Nations had decided to use force on behalf of the central government to unify the country. This went against a basic principle that the Secretary-General had upheld from the very beginning.

Hammarskjöld first learned that something had gone wrong during a refueling stop at Accra where he read a Reuters dispatch about the fighting and quoting O'Brien. After reaching Leopoldville he wasted no time in re-criminations or rebukes and set about trying to retrieve the situation.

There was no turn for the better during the next three days. Attacks on the UN troops continued in Katanga and efforts to make contact with Tshombe were un-availing. In Leopoldville the parliament unanimously voted in favour of launching an invasion of Katanga.

Strong protests, partly based on misinformation about UN intentions, were directed to the Secretary-General from London, Washington, and Brussels. Finally, on September 16 O'Brien received word through the British consul in Elisabethville that Tshombe would talk with him the next day in Bancroft, Northern Rhodesia, across the border from Katanga. Hammarskjöld trans-mitted at once the message that follows proposing that he himself fly to meet Tshombe on September 17 at Ndola instead, where there was an airport.

»The proposed meeting obviously requires that or-ders should be given beforehand for an immediate and effective cease-fire. [...] The ceasefire will occur auto-matically on the United Nations side, in view of the fact that according to the instructions given and the rules followed by the Organization, it only opens fire in self-defence. »[...]

Tshombe replied during the morning of September 17 that he agreed in principle to an immediate cease-fire but demanded that UN troops be confined to their camps and that all troop movements and reinforcements by ground or air be suspended. These conditions were, of course, unacceptable and the Secretary-General sent an immediate response that only unconditional ceasefire could make a condition for the meeting. /.../

When O'Brien passed on this message to the British consul he was told that Tshombe was about to leave his Northern Rhodesian refuge for Ndola. Hammarskjöld then decided to go himself without waiting for a reply in order not to lose any more time. His DC-6B plane took off just before 5 p.m. local time. With the Secretary-General were Heinrich Wieschhoff, his principal adviser on Africa, William Ranallo, his personal aide, Vladimir Fabry, Linnér's legal adviser, a secretary and three security officers borrowed from ONUC, and two Swedish UN soldiers. There was a six-man Swedish crew.

Because of the Fouga jet no flight plan was filed beyond Luluabourg and the plane observed radio silence for most of the trip. Late in the evening it made radio contact with the Ndola control tower and at ten minutes after midnight local time informed the tower that the airfield lights were in sight and it was descending. An instruction to report when it reached 6 000 ft. above sea level was acknowledged. Thereafter there was silence.

Not until the next afternoon, fifteen hours later, was the wreckage sighted, about ten miles from the airport. The plane had crashed and disintegrated in flames in a wooded area. The rescue party found only one man alive, Harold Julien, one of the UN security men. He had been terribly burned and died a few days later without being able to give any information on the circumstances of the disaster.

Hammarskjöld had been thrown clear of the wreckage and was the only victim not burned at all, but he had suffered massive and surely fatal internal injuries. Because of the circumstances in which the flight had been undertaken there were widespread suspicions of sabotage or some other form of foul play. A UN investigation commission later found no evidence to support such theories but also reported its inability definitely to exclude any of four possible causes – sabotage, attack from ground or air, aircraft failure, or pilot failure. One fact was clear. The plane was on a normal landing approach to the airport, with wheels and wing flaps lowered. For whatever reason, it had been a few feet too low to clear the trees on rising ground beneath it.

The Secretary-General's chair on the podium stood empty when the General Assembly began its sixteenth annual session on September 19. In Ndola the next day Tshombe concluded with Khiari a cease-fire agreement after first laying a wreath on Hammarskjöld's coffin. (The ceasefire did not last long and there were to be further episodes of violence before the secession of Katanga finally came to an end in January 1963).

A chartered plane then began the last flight home, with brief stops along the way at Leopoldville and Geneva. Sweden was in full mourning and on September 28 the King and Queen led a throng of notables from all over the world at a state funeral in the Cathedral of Uppsala and then to the Hammarskjöld family plot in the old graveyard where the Secretary-General found his resting place. A few weeks later the Norwegian parliament announced the posthumous award of the Nobel Peace Prize to Dag Hammarskjöld.

After the plane crash Hammarskjöld's briefcase was found intact near his body. Besides the small copy of the United Nations Charter and an English edition of the New Testament and Psalms which were always with him when he traveled, was a copy of a new edition of Martin Buber's Ich und Du (I and Thou) and a legal size yellow writing pad which Hammarskjöld used during the flight to continue work on a Swedish translation of the Jewish philosopher's book that he had begun only a few days earlier.

Among the effects the Secretary-General had left in his room in Linnér's house at Leopoldville when he departed on the flight to Ndola were the first twelve typed pages of his translation of Ich und Du with handwritten corrections on the first page. There was also a typed copy of an article he had written during the summer of 1961 for publication in the 1962 Yearbook of the Swedish Tourist Association. It was entitled Slottsbacken (Castle Hill) and was written in response to a request for his recollections of the Uppsala of his student days, when his father was governor of the province and he lived in the castle on the hill. He set down his memories of those days in the order of the four seasons, a series of sensitive word pictures evoking the cycle of nature and the life of the town and its people through the year – by turns merry, compassionate, reflective. Of the time just before New Year's he wrote: »The Lutheran hymns' reminder of time's bitter flight and the transience of all things captures the mood in which the Castle has sunk back while winter darkness has deepened. When the wind sweeps in from the plain against the walls one remembers the words of the old, that a windy new year's eve bodes the death of great men.«